Hilda M. Miske
141 S. Park Lane N.E.
Grand Rapids, Mich.

LEE AFTER THE WAR

OTHER BOOKS BY MARSHALL W. FISHWICK

Gentlemen of Virginia

Sleeping Beauty and Her Suitors:
The South in the Sixties

Virginia: A New Look at the Old Dominion

The Virginia Tradition

American Heroes: Myth and Reality

General Lee's Photographer

Rockbridge County, Virginia:
An Informal History

Virginians on Olympus

The Face of Jang

Isle of Shoals

LEE
AFTER THE WAR

MARSHALL W. FISHWICK

ILLUSTRATED

DODD, MEAD & COMPANY
NEW YORK

Copyright © 1963 by Marshall W. Fishwick

All rights reserved

No part of this book may be reproduced in any form
without permission in writing from the publisher

Library of Congress Catalog Card Number: 63-10239

Printed in the United States of America
by The Haddon Craftsmen, Inc., Scranton, Pennsylvania

Acknowledgment is gratefully made to Mr. Donald Davidson for permission to quote from *Lee in the Mountains*, and to Brandt and Brandt for permission to quote from Stephen Vincent Benét's *John Brown's Body* (Copyright, 1927, 1928, by Stephen Vincent Benét. Copyright renewed, 1955, 1956, by Rosemary Carr Benét).

To
Jeff, Ellie, Sue, and Lou—
raised on General Lee's campus

ACKNOWLEDGMENTS

No American can hope to thank all those who have made his heritage come alive. No Southerner knows just where and when Lee took on for him heroic proportions. Still, I am aware of the tremendous debt I owe these people, which I hereby acknowledge with gratitude:

Douglas Southall Freeman, who shared his books and unmatched erudition with me;

James Branch Cabell, who believed all nice people should say naughty things about sacred cows, just to balance the record;

Clayton Torrence, who first published my meager efforts in the area of Virginiana;

Francis P. Gaines, whose eloquent words made Lee live;

My colleagues at Washington and Lee University, who were generous with their time and comments;

Ralph Gabriel, who encouraged me to study the Lee legend in graduate school;

William Poole, who edited my manuscript with unlimited skill and patience;

Professor Frank Vandiver, who kindly read the whole manuscript, and made valuable suggestions;

Mrs. Alta Feddeman, for her notable skill and diligence with the preparation of the manuscript in its various stages.

From such people, inspiration is a free and fortunate gift which we cannot hope either to merit or to repay.

Most of the photographs used were made by the nineteenth century photographer, Michael Miley. His priceless collection of glass plates is now owned by the Virginia Historical Society, which has graciously approved of their being used. Thanks are due also to the Rockbridge Historical Society for use of their fine photographs.

—Marshall W. Fishwick

PROLOGUE

My home is on the Washington and Lee University campus. Close by is the Chapel, a small building of dubious aesthetic distinction. Yet visitors come there daily, in good weather and bad. Bus loads of children arrive and enter quietly. This is a shrine. Robert E. Lee is buried here.

His life has been recorded so minutely and his career praised so lavishly that one feels he should explain why he has dared to write another Lee book. Hasn't his story been told, often and well?

It is not the story of Lee, but the meaning of Lee, that I am writing about. Do not expect to find in this little book much that Douglas Southall Freeman omitted from his four huge volumes. Still, the world (and especially the American South) is a very different place from the one in which Freeman wrote thirty years ago. Lee's battle plans for Gettysburg have not changed, but we have. What does Lee mean for us in a world of missiles and astronauts?

Plainly, my study is more impressionistic than scientific. I cannot examine Lee clinically: I am enthralled by him. At the same time, I have tried to use the most accurate information available. Having spent the last decade where Lee lived out his life after Appomattox, I have tried to use local sources and sights which other biographers have missed.

To see Lee the man, we must get past Lee the Guardian Angel. This is no easy task, especially in Lexington. I do not think he has gained from this apotheosis. To dehumanize and elevate by excessive adulation, and to invoke his name for many latter-day Lost Causes, does no honor to the man. To know the human Lee is to admire him. He was not the kind of man to demand even that much, let alone more.

MARSHALL W. FISHWICK

Lexington, Virginia

CONTENTS

	Prologue	ix
1.	THE ENTRANCE	1
2.	THE EXIT	20
3.	THE PHOTOGRAPH	36
4.	THE LETTER	48
5.	THE VALLEY	62
6.	THE TOWN	75
7.	THE RITUAL	88
8.	THE HEARING	108
9.	THE OFFICE	128
10.	THE WEDDING	146
11.	THE LONG WINTER	161
12.	THE STROLL	173
13.	THE TREK	184
14.	THE VESTRY MEETING	202
15.	THE VIGIL	216
16.	THE GUARDIAN ANGEL	222
	Bibliographical Note	231
	Index	235

ILLUSTRATIONS

Following page 114

Washington College, 1868
Lee's letter accepting the presidency of Washington College
General Francis Smith, president of V.M.I.
Brady's picture of Lee and his son Custis
Lee on Traveller
The Lees' Lexington living room
Mrs. Robert E. Lee
Lee's Washington College office
Lee's campus home
Old mill near Lexington
Lexington's Main Street
Lee's funeral procession
Campus on the day Lee was buried
Friends of Robert E. Lee
Valentine's statue of Lee
Last photograph of Lee by Miley

Can anyone say that they know Robert E. Lee?
                            —Mary Boykin Chestnut

It is not General Lee, young man.
It is Robert Lee in a dark civilian suit who walks,
An outlaw fumbling for the latch, a voice
Commanding in a dream where no flag flies.
                            —Donald Davidson

I

THE ENTRANCE

> There was silence deep as death,
> And the boldest held his breath,
> For a time.
> —Thomas Campbell

THAT EASTER EVE a soft redemptive rain fell on Richmond, Virginia. Thousands of tears were added to millions of raindrops. Caught between Friday and Sunday, men thought more of death than of resurrection.

April 15, 1865. General Robert E. Lee crossed the makeshift pontoon bridge over the James River and entered the charred capital. "Richmond must not be given up," he had once said, "it *shall not* be given up." Now it was grim and gutted. On Palm Sunday he had faced the humiliation of Appomattox. On Easter he would dwell in the ashes of Richmond.

"As Lee passed," an observer recalled, "a deep murmur rose from the very heart of the crowd." Removing his soggy gray hat, the General bowed gravely. The sword of Lee rested in the scabbard. Removing it this night, he would never don it again.

Shortly before, in a little town along the James, a Baptist minister had glanced out at the gloomy landscape and seen Lee riding by. "His steed was spattered with mud, and his head hung as if worn by long traveling," William Hatcher wrote. "His face was ridged with self-respecting grief. I was awed by his incomparable dignity."

Once proud and imperial, Richmond was a center of desolation—a melancholy wasteland in which empty streets were blanketed by rubble and ashes. The heart of the Confederacy had stopped beating. Scrawny women, jaundiced old men and ragged children stood on the corners, begging alms from the conquerors. Bony arms and imploring eyes told more about the fate of Richmond than all the official reports. Behold the ruins: factories, mills, warehouses, arsenals, stores, foundries, bridges, railroad yards. The air itself seemed paralyzed. The Easter sun would rise on mountains of rubbish, blackened walls and impassable streets. Hardly a brick wall stood more than shoulder high.

Only a small wooden sign—LIBBY PRISON—identified an infamous building where misery and starvation had long dwelled. On the same memory-soaked street, prisoners peered through iron bars. Confined or free, Richmonders had no place to go. For cities, as for men, there is a point beyond which no hope penetrates. Lee sensed and saw this as he rode slowly forward. He saw more. Trained to scan landscapes, he saw, across the city, the spire of Saint Paul's Church, a clean stiletto piercing the glum sky.

Down Main Street the small party went, soiled, sad-hearted, heading for what would be Lee's temporary home:

707 East Franklin Street. Owned by John Stewart of Brook Hill, the plain brick structure had a symmetrical façade and a white neo-classical porch. It had been rented by Lee's son Custis when the latter was on President Davis' staff. Soon afterwards, Mrs. Robert E. Lee and her daughters moved in too. Once the war ended, the Lees insisted on paying a more ample rent.

"You owe me nothing," Stewart replied. "If you insist on paying, it must be in Confederate currency, as we originally agreed." Thus the house was rent-free: Confederate money was worthless. This arrangement the Lees would accept no longer than was absolutely necessary.

At this moment, however, the General who had endured four years in the field must have thought primarily of the mere existence of a dwelling—four walls, hearth, the sense of having his family together under one roof. Would he find here the renewal and strength and spirit on which mere survival depended?

Actually we will never know what Robert E. Lee was thinking when he went up the stone steps on Franklin Street that rainy Saturday in 1865; but historians will never stop wondering about his thoughts.

What a winter he had just passed through! Month after month, day after day, defeat and disaster had broken like wild waves on a stormy beach, pounding like the doomsday drum. Ever since Gettysburg, Lee had faced the inevitable outcome. Those who knew less could hope for more. Not that the South was willing to surrender. Why should it, with Robert E. Lee in the field? The Gray Fox and his sinew-tough Army of Northern Virginia had broken out of traps before. The hounds would have some howling and some bleeding to do before the hunt was over.

Blue and gray, "Bluebelly" and "Butternut," old and young, this was a bitter time. Red blood covered the white snow. Death was everywhere: dead men, dead dreams, dead phrases. Among the many galloping horses were four that would not and could not be bridled—Death, Famine, Pestilence, and Murder.

Amidst all the bloody drama stood three principal actors: Lincoln, Grant, and Lee—the battered emancipator, the barrel-chested attacker, and the aristocratic defender. Each did what he thought he had to do, respectful of the others, aware of his own enormous power. Pompous politicians and ambitious schemers trailed the trio like lewd camp followers. Soldiers with soaring ambitions tried to dash ahead of them. But no one could push this trio from the center of the stage. Theirs were the main roles in the drama. The fifth act came in the spring of 1865.

General Grant welcomed the climax. He spurred history as he would a disobedient colt. From the ancient geometers he had learned that a straight line was the shortest distance between two points. When, during the winter of 1865 Butler forgot this, he removed him from command of the Army of the James and put in Ord. The way to destroy the Confederacy was to roll Lee back—whatever the cost—like a carpet.

"Our country is now environed with perils which it is our duty calmly to contemplate," said Jefferson Davis. That duty alone might not overcome those perils never seemed to have occurred to him. He overestimated everything Confederate, especially himself. But there was no limit to his courage and integrity. Sherman's march through Georgia and the Carolinas did not shake his faith; neither did Sheridan's devastation of the rich Shenandoah Valley. By March the Confederate price of flour had reached $1,500 in many places. Not cannon but hunger, inflation, and exhaustion would destroy the nation of which Davis was destined to be the first and only president.

In Richmond the politicians mouthed the brave old phrases, but they did not comment on the plight of the Confederate army. Of the estimated 600,000 Southern troops in the field in 1863, over half of those still alive by the winter of 1865 had left the ranks. Those that remained came gradually to replace the dream of victory with the vision of fire. Dixie would die, as she had lived, in the grand manner. *Gotterdammerung.*

Desperately short of men—he had only 1,100 to the mile outside Petersburg—Lee favored employing slaves as soldiers, freeing any who would enlist. Diehards in the Confederate Congress tried to push the idea aside. On January 13, news came that General Hood, retreating into Mississippi, had sent his resignation of command to Richmond. That same day the North captured Wilmington, North Carolina. The last remaining Confederate port of the eastern seaboard was closed.

Now the Northern foe was ready to reconquer Charleston, South Carolina. The Stars and Stripes flew again over Fort Sumter, four years after being dragged down. The rebels had been purged and punished; good had been burned with evil. Words of the Yankee battle hymn had been fulfilled:

> He is trampling out the vintage where the grapes of wrath are stored;
> He hath loosed the fateful lightning of his terrible swift sword . . .

On January 19, 1865, his fifty-eighth birthday, General Lee was made Commander in Chief of the Armies of the Confederate States. Too late. That same day Sherman left Savannah and moved toward North Carolina. The Confederacy was collapsing.

Saturated with destruction, the whole region for miles was a broad black streak of ruin. Lonesome smoke stacks, surrounded by heaps of ashes and cinders, marked the spot where plantations and cities had stood. In place of crops were weeds. Still Lee held out. As long as he led, his tatterdemalions would follow.

Grant was jumpy. "One of the most anxious periods of my experience during the Rebellion was the last weeks before Petersburg," he wrote in his memoirs. "I was afraid, every morning, that I would awake from my sleep to hear that Lee had gone and nothing was left but a picket line."

In nearby Richmond, President Davis, standing in the quiet eye of the hurricane, still expected victory. If necessary, he would defend the capital himself. Not one note of humility crept into his last dispatches; not one indication of the compassion that might have allowed him to assume the role of the tragic hero. Was it pride or latent fear that gripped him in that dreadful winter? Probably both. The oncoming Yankee troops sang:

> We'll hang Jeff Davis on a sour apple tree
> As we go marching on.

In the North, the Republican Party had busied itself getting Abraham Lincoln reelected and the Thirteenth Amendment abolishing slavery adopted. On January 31, the measure passed in the House of Representatives. The vote was one hundred nineteen to fifty-six. The response of the densely packed gallery, wrote a correspondent, "surpassed all precedent and beggared all description."

At that moment, at the other end of Pennsylvania Avenue, President Lincoln was writing a directive to Secretary of State William Seward: "You will proceed to Fortress Monroe, Virginia, there to meet and informally confer with representatives of the Confederacy. You will make known to them that three things are indispensable . . ." But the South was not ready to give up the struggle—yet.

Lee, however, had no stomach for slaughter just for the sake of slaughter. On March 2 he wrote General Grant, requesting a conference to consider a settlement of difficulties in regard to prisoners and hospitals. Grant declined, as Lincoln had instructed him to, unless the proposal was surrender. Always obedient to civil authority, Lee had no alternative now. He must stretch his defensive line until it broke.

At noon two days later, Abraham Lincoln was sworn in for a second Presidential term that would expire in 1869. In the North, cannon boomed, crowds cheered, and men asked when the war would be over.

"May he live to see the nation under his Administration at peace," wrote the Illinois *State Journal*, "and all the more prosperous because in the past he has been true to Freedom and Union."

"This is a great day in Yankeedom," the Petersburg *Daily Express* wrote bitterly. "Emperor Abraham's coronation is to come off in the Capitol . . . What is it to him or them that war devours its hecatombs of victims? Did not Nero fiddle whilst Rome was burning?"

The Confederate Congress in a pathetic defiant gesture

adopted a new flag that afternoon. Time was running out. Flag-waving days in the South were almost over.

In Washington, Chief Justice Chase administered the oath to Lincoln and his new Vice President, Andrew Johnson. Then came words, simple and spiritual, such as no other President had ever used to speak to the people: "With malice towards none; with charity for all; with firmness in the right, as God gives us to see the right, let us strive on to finish the work we are in; to bind the nation's wounds; to care for him who shall have borne the battle, and for his widow and his orphan . . ."

Grant, who could discipline his men, his officers, and his tongue, kept pushing. Having served from the Missouri River to the James and bagged whole armies at Fort Donelson and Vicksburg, he knew that the final Northern victory hinged on the surrender of Lee. Peach blooms and apricot blossoms were bursting out in Tidewater Virginia when Lincoln stepped ashore at City Point, Virginia, on March 29. The President and his barrel-chested general talked of how the carnage might be ended. Grant told of a suggestion to supply the Federals with bayonets a foot longer than the enemy's: "Then when they met, our bayonets would go clear through the enemy, while theirs would not reach far enough to touch our men, and the war would be ended."

"Well, there is a good deal of terror in steel," Lincoln said. "I had a chance to test it once myself." However, he instructed Grant to do all he could to avoid a final bloody battle.

In April the Confederacy sank into the shadows and the dusk.

On April 1, camped outside Petersburg, Grant wrote: "Today our troops under Sheridan went over the parapets of the enemy. The two armies were mingled together there for a time in such a manner that it was almost a question which one was going to demand the surrender of the other. The enemy broke and ran in every direction."

The Rebel right had been turned. Over 3200 Confederate prisoners were taken. The next morning Lee abandoned his positions and led his gaunt remnant to the west. If he could reach Lynchburg and the railroad, he might somehow link up with General Johnston. Or perhaps he could retreat into the mountains and fight guerrilla-style until a new army could be formed. That was how General Washington had won his rebellion.

The Sunday morning service at Saint Paul's Church, Richmond, was interrupted by a mud-splattered courier who held his saber so it would not rattle as he walked up the aisle to deliver an urgent message to President Davis. The Reverend Mr. Minnegerode paused, then continued with the service of Morning Prayer. Everyone guessed what the message portended. It said: "I will advise you later, according to circumstances."

Mr. Davis left church and sent a sharp reply to General Lee, complaining that a night exit "would involve the loss of many valuables, both for the want of time to pack and of transportation." Lee, who had strained every nerve and every man to hold out this long, tore the telegram to bits. He had given all the notice he could.

In spite of his protests, the President abandoned Richmond at eleven o'clock that night. Moving by rail to Danville, he set up a temporary capital and urged Southerners "to enter a new phase of the struggle." Abandoned and doomed, Richmond faced the worst day in its history as the Sabbath sun rose on April 2. Captain Clement Sulivane, in charge of the evacuation, tried to keep order but soon gave up. Battalions melted away as soon as they were formed. So did law and order. Looting, burning, dynamiting and destruction followed. A battalion of naval cadets marched with fixed bayonets, escorting the treasury to safety. Piles of new unsigned money burned in front of Jefferson's capital building. Government bonds drifted around the streets like confetti. Mobs pushed and gouged their way to the one bridge left standing over the James.

The Confederate government gave orders to burn all tobacco and cotton that could not be removed so that the Yankees could not capture it. Flaming balls of tar turned the waterfront into a bonfire. In one warehouse, Shockoe's, over ten thousand hogsheads went up. Brisk breezes scattered sparks and embers everywhere. Powder magazines and arsenals exploded with whooshing booms. A cascade of red-hot metal covered Richmond.

At daybreak on April 3, thousands of people invaded the commissary depot. Half-starved for months, they wanted plunder and provisions before the Yankees arrived. Cursing, crying, raging, snarling, the mob took over. Barrels of liquor were smashed open. When officials ordered all whisky destroyed and it flooded the gutters, white and colored people filled their pitchers or got on their knees to drink like animals. The air was filled with yells, cries of distress, and horrid songs. Soldiers fired tar and pitch balls onto the roofs of buildings, churches and homes. Fortunately, some of these balls—like the one that landed on the Lees' roof—did not ignite.

Down at the bridge, General Gary was watching his last

soldiers dash across the bridge. "All right, Captain," he said to Sulivane as the last one crossed, "blow her to hell!"

At dawn on April 3, the Fourth Massachusetts Cavalry entered the beleaguered city. That morning, at the City Hall, General Godfrey Weitzel received the surrender of Richmond. To contain the fire, the Yankees blew up buildings in its path, adding to the inferno. Not all who saw it wept. "I have cried until no more tears will come," one Richmond lady said.

Trying desperately to elude his vastly stronger foe, Lee had no time to visit or think of Richmond. But on April 4, President Lincoln boarded the S.S. *Malvern* and steamed toward the fallen city. Dead horses, abandoned barges, and broken ordnance littered the river. When the ship ran aground, Admiral Porter shifted the President to a twelve-oared barge which took him to the edge of Richmond. A large group of Negroes awaited him on the shore.

"Bress de Lawd, dere is de great Messiah!" one of them yelled. "He's bin in my heart fo' long yeahs. Glory, hallelujah!" He and others fell on their knees as Lincoln approached.

"Don't kneel to me," he said. "You must kneel to God only and thank Him for your freedom."

Entering the city, Lincoln paused a moment to gaze at Libby Prison. "Tear it down!" someone shouted.

"No, leave it as a monument," Lincoln replied. After a two-mile walk, Lincoln reached the Confederate Executive Mansion, pale, haggard, utterly worn out. His first words were: "I wonder if I could get a glass of water."

Soon Lincoln was back on the *Malvern*, with memories that must have been as painful as bayonet wounds. For on the night after he returned to City Point, President Lincoln had a terrible nightmare. He dreamed that the White House was burning up.

So were Lee's supplies and his fading hopes. The Yankees were closing in. There was no way to stop them. Wrote General Grant to his wife: "The suffering which must exist in the South next year will be beyond calculation."

Lee lurched westward. Everybody that had a horse was in the saddle. About 28,000 Confederates were still in the field. "You are the country to these men," one of Lee's officers told him. "They have fought on for you without pay or clothes, or care of any sort. Their devotion to you and faith in you have been the only things which have held this army together."

A curious elation gripped the overtaxed Confederates. "Come on!" one of them yelled to his comrades as the Yankees closed in, "you want to live forever?" Lee who had worked so many miracles might perform still another one; General Joseph Johnston was only 107 miles away. While their starved horses gnawed tree bark and they themselves munched dried corn, the soldiers in gray sang:

> The race is not to them that's got
> The longest legs to run,
> Nor the battle to that people
> That shoots the biggest gun.

On they trudged, impelled by some blind glory of the human soul, lashing out at the inevitable growing darkness. But at Amelia Courthouse, a new threat developed: starvation. Supply had completely broken down. Not a single ration for man or beast was on hand. Lee had to squander his precious one-day lead over the Yankees by foraging for food. Out the wagons went. On a soggy rainy April 5 they returned—almost empty. The farmers had nothing to give or sell. The land had already been stripped clean.

That was not the worst news. Later that day, Lee learned that Federal troops were firmly entrenched in his line of advance, seven miles from Amelia. The escape route was blocked. Forlorn and famished, soldiers left ranks by battalions. The limits of flesh and blood had been reached.

On April 6, the still defiant Lee rode up on a ridge. He saw—streaming out of the bottom and up the ridge—teamsters without wagons, soldiers without guns, shattered regiments without officers.

"My God!" he cried as if to himself, "has the army been dissolved?"

Spurring Traveller, Lee rushed forward, took hold of a battle flag and held it aloft. His soldiers, hysterical with fear, hunger, and pain, drew around him as if to be sheltered by his regnant calm. This was the last rally the Army of Northern Virginia ever made. What had been a fighting force was becoming a routed wreck, an unarmed mob seeking food.

The entire country, North and South, waited tensely for news of the climactic hostilities. Most Southerners had no more faith in their government, but they knew that Robert E. Lee was still in command. Grant, who was getting frequent messages from his advancing generals, tried to keep the White House informed as the situation changed rapidly. A wire sent to Washington at midnight, April 6, told of the wholesale capture of Confederates, including General Lee's son Custis and Generals Ewell, Kershaw, Button and Corse. Grant quoted a line from Sheridan's dispatch: "If the thing is pressed, I think that Lee will surrender."

The long-weary and now almost victorious Lincoln read the midnight message and let Grant know what he thought must be done: "General Sheridan says, 'If the thing is pressed I think that Lee will surrender.' Let the thing be pressed."

Pressed it was, hour after hour, over roads and fields that had become deathtraps. Years later, Allen Tate would invite us to look with awe at the scene:

> Turn your eyes to the inscrutable infantry rising
> Demons out of the earth—they will not last.

The story was written along the roads, littered like a beach with driftwood from a fast-ebbing tide: broken guns, discarded muskets and bedrolls, horses collapsed from utter exhaustion, abandoned wagons and ambulances, stragglers stumbling listlessly along or falling in ditches. Close by was General Sheridan's well-fed, victory-sure Northern cavalry —wheeling and dashing, ready for the final victory which had eluded them so long. Occasionally the air was pierced by a spine-tingling Rebel yell—a last note of defiance.

Every report that reached Lee indicated that the end was in sight. "I've fought my corps to a frazzle and I can do nothing unless Longstreet can support me," Colonel Charles Venable told Lee. "Old Pete" Longstreet had nothing to support him with. Was guerrilla warfare a possibility? "We'll scatter like rabbits and partridges in the woods, and fight on for years," an officer suggested.

Lee said no. "There is nothing left me but to go and see General Grant," he said.

"Oh, General, what will history say of the surrender of the army in the field?" an aide asked.

"Yes, I know they will say hard things of us; they will not understand how we were overwhelmed by numbers; but that is not the question, Colonel; the question is, is it right to surrender this army? If it is right, then I will take the responsibility."

April 9, Palm Sunday, was a sharp, clear Virginia day. Tender, sticky buds covered the trees. The air, balmy and fragrant, smelled of springtime. Oak trees were covered with long yellow tassels. Where gardens had once bloomed were clumps of weeds. An occasional hyacinth or snowdrop managed to peep through. Heavy guns had crushed the tender bulbs. Spring would have to soothe the multiple scars with her gentle fingertips. Sweet-singing birds would obliterate bitter memories.

Just a week earlier, the valiant General A. P. Hill had been shot down after the Petersburg break-through. When he had heard the news, Lee's eyes filled with tears. "He is at rest now," Lee had murmured, "and we who are left are the ones to suffer." On Palm Sunday General Lee said in a loud enough voice so that his staff could hear him: "How easily I could be rid of this, and be at rest. I have only to ride along the line and all will be over . . ."

Nothing in or about him favored selfish solutions. So he returned to his quarters to don a spotless new uniform, boots embroidered in red silk, buckskin gauntlets and a soft gray felt hat with a golden cord. To his side he buckled his jeweled sword crowned with the head of a lion, housed in a gilt-trimmed scabbard. Virginia had presented it to him.

So Robert E. Lee went, as he knew he must, to surrender to Ulysses S. Grant, a man in well-worn, mud-spattered boots and breeches, whose three-starred shoulder straps were the lone indicators of his rank.

And about three forty-five that afternoon, in the home of

Wilmer McLean, Lee signed the surrender paper with no outward show of emotion.

Later on, as he waited for an orderly to replace his horse's bridle, Lee breathed a sigh that was almost deep enough to be a groan. In his mind the guns must still have echoed; the graves were still being dug; the tears were still being shed. The load he had carried was too heavy to be set aside now, no matter what documents were signed.

The terms and treatment, however, had been generous. Lee had told Grant they would be "very gratifying, and do much toward the reconciliation of our people."

Now Grant added one last small touch of respect, providing the right coda for Appomattox. As Lee rode away, Grant stepped down from the McLean porch, took off his hat and stood in silence. So did his battle-hardened staff. There is no single greater act of military tribute in American history.

Now that all seemed lost, Lee did not look for a scapegoat. Nor did he conceal his own innate and very Virginian pride, which an earlier aristocrat, Thomas Jefferson, had decided "costs us more than hunger or cold." Of the collapsed Southern cause, Lee said, "It was all my fault. I thought my men were invincible."

Yet not all was lost at Appomattox. Those who stacked their arms and battle flags emerged with more than the bootless glory of battle. From the ashes and anguish they extracted a handful of immutable memories. Ashes and memories, well mixed, make a potent medicine.

Facing his own men on April 9 was harder for Lee than facing Grant's. "Blow, Gabriel, blow!" one Rebel cried. "Let him blow. I am ready to die." Some blubbered and blasphemed. Grim, bearded veterans fell to the ground, covered their faces and wept. Officers on both sides, many of whom had served together in the years before 1861, met again, enjoying the comradeship that fighting men share, no matter what color their uniforms. When final greetings and farewells were being given, Lee talked with General Meade, his opponent at Gettysburg. As the pair rode toward Confederate headquarters, Meade had his color bearer unfurl the Stars and Stripes as cheers came from the Confederate lines. "Down with your old rag!" a lean veteran said from the roadside, "we are cheering General Lee."

In his last General Order, Lee expressed "unceasing admiration" for these men and their devotion. Now he would no longer be a commanding general, but as Donald Davidson would put it:

> An outlaw fumbling for the latch, a voice
> Commanding in a dream where no flag flies.

That afternoon Lee retired to a nearby apple orchard to pace back and forth nervously. "His staff kept at a distance except to present visitors," the Confederate officer, W. W. Blackford, wrote. "General Lee shook hands with none of them. He would halt in his pacing and stand at attention and glare at them with a look few men could assume. Near sunset Lee left the orchard and rode to his headquarters."

Lee stayed on for two days, to share with his men the grief and shock of surrender, to receive his staff's final reports, and to write his own. Meticulous and official to the end, he explained the army's final collapse in a single sentence: "We had no subsistence for man or horse, and it could not be gathered in the country." From the information available to him, he concluded that at the time of surrender he had only 7,892 infantrymen bearing arms and sixty-three pieces of artillery.

With as little ceremony as possible, Lee and three aides started for Richmond on Wednesday morning, April 12. With them went a battered ambulance, captured from General Banks in Second Manassas days, and a baggage wagon on which a bedquilt served as the canvas tilt. Lee rode Traveller, the mount that had carried him throughout the war.

The barren landscape—the very ground they had passed over so recently—must have depressed the four men beyond measure. All was quiet now, but it was the peace of desolation. The earth was pockmarked with gopher holes, scratched out by men who smelled death in the air. Hardly a fence, chicken, horse or cow could be seen. In place of men covered with dirt and powder, chimneys blackened by fire stood as silent sentries. Carcasses of dead animals polluted the air. From the sky came the hideous, bleak croak of vultures, anticipating their feast. Weeds and brambles, having choked out the crops, were outdone only by the stiff, uncompromising pines. Roads showed deep scars and endless litter. Occasionally part of a body had been washed out of a shallow grave . . . an arm, a foot, or a face whose sightless eyes stared at the sky.

Being a churchman, Lee must have recalled that this was Holy Week; that Golgotha, the Hill of Skulls, could not have been much worse than this. He, too, would have his own particular cross to bear. Burned black stumps were the death-like milestones of the journey home.

Each spring for years later, in these fields, farmers would turn up a new crop of bullets and bones. Moss-tufted earthworks would remain where men had burrowed into the ground like moles. Those who had been lucky enough to fight and live on would remember for years. The landscape would remember for decades.

Farm families greeted Lee, spoke to him, wept quietly. That night the little party stopped two miles east of Buckingham Courthouse, pitching its tents in the woods. Thursday morning saw Colonel Venable turn southward toward his home. Moving on to Cumberland Courthouse, the others spent the night at Flanagan's Mill. Having lost a shoe, Traveller was shod. Early Friday saw the trek underway again. In the afternoon they reached the home of General Lee's brother in Powhatan County. The General surrendered his room to a sick officer and his wife and pitched his tent close by. This was the last night he ever slept under canvas. On the ground he loved so much and had defended so well, Lee lay down and thought his own thoughts. Good Friday drew to an end.

He could not know that, as he closed his eyes on Carter Lee's plantation, his great adversary, Abraham Lincoln, was closing his in Ford's Theater in Washington. He could not know that before he entered Richmond on April 15, Lincoln would leave the world and the people whom he had served so well. Much darkness lay in the immediate past for Lee and his people; and much more darkness lay ahead.

II

THE EXIT

> The purple lilacs bloomed April the Fourteenth
> of the year Eighteen Sixty-Five.
> And the shining air held a balance of miracles
> good and evil.
> —Carl Sandburg

On the eve of Palm Sunday, 1865, Abraham Lincoln boarded the steamer *River Queen* at City Point, Virginia, to return to Washington, D.C.

The trip just ending seemed to some his most courageous, to others his most foolhardy, venture. While Rebel buildings and tempers were still inflamed, he had walked through the streets of Richmond, unarmed and practically unguarded. He wanted to show, as well as to preach, a spirit of reconciliation. No substitute would do. The master of the Federal White House wanted to stand in the Confederate White House—not to gloat over the vanquished, but to demonstrate that the Union had been preserved. This he had done. Now he could go home.

A military band was present for his departure. After several army ditties, the bandmaster asked the Chief Executive if he had any special requests. "Yes," Lincoln replied. "Play 'Dixie.' Let the people know that they are free to hear it again."

The song and the palms of victory were pleasant and good to Abraham Lincoln on that Palm Sunday. While Robert E. Lee told his men of the loss, Lincoln went home to speak of the victory. After years of anguish, defeat and frustration, it must have seemed more like a fond wish than a reality. Was the Union really preserved? Had Old Abe seen the thing through?

Slouching comfortably in a deck chair as evening cloaked the James River, more relaxed than he had been for years, Lincoln knew that the most difficult part of the job was ahead: "to bind up the nation's wounds, to care for him who shall have borne the battle, and for his widow and his orphan —to do all which may achieve and cherish a just and lasting peace among ourselves and with all nations."

Having resisted the cries of rebellion, he was equally determined to stand firm against the voices that cried out for revenge. Dixie was to be helped quickly to her feet, not ground under heel. The blood bath was over.

On board with the President were his wife and several important politicians, including Senator Charles Pineton and the Marquis de Chambrun. His detailed diary recreates the trip vividly. Most of Palm Sunday, he tells us, was spent talking of literary subjects. "Mr. Lincoln read us for several hours passages from Shakespeare. Most of these were from *Macbeth*—in particular, the verses which follow Duncan's assassination:

'Duncan is in his grave;
After life's fitful fever he sleeps well;
Treason has done his worst; nor steel, nor poison,
Malice domestic, foreign levy, nothing
Can touch him further—'

Holding a quarto of Shakespeare in his hands, Lincoln paused and commented how true a description of the murderer that was, when, the dark deed achieved, its tortured perpetrator came to envy his victim's sleep. Then he went back and read it a second time.

No effort to keep the conversation off politics could succeed entirely on such a trip. Somehow the name of Jefferson Davis came up. "Do not allow him to escape the law," snapped Mrs. Lincoln who did not share her husband's magnanimity and greatness of soul. "He must be hanged!"

Lincoln did not argue with her. He simply quoted seven lines of Scripture beginning with: "Judge not, that ye be not judged."

Shortly after that, the steamer chugged past Mount Vernon, home and final resting place of George Washington. "Mount Vernon and Springfield, the memories of Washington and your own; these are the spots and names America shall one day equally honor," the perceptive young French nobleman said to Lincoln as they gazed ashore.

"Springfield!" Lincoln replied. "How happy, four years hence, I will be to return there in peace and tranquility."

It is well that no human eye can pierce the veil of history. Otherwise, our triumphs would be as nothing, fronted with glimpses of fleeting and whimsical existence. What sort of trip would it have been on the *River Queen* if the passengers had known that Lincoln, who had escaped harm in antagonistic Richmond, would soon be assassinated in friendly Washington?

Moving so effortlessly and quietly from Richmond to Washington along a river fought over so desperately, Lincoln must have felt deep inner satisfaction on that warm Sabbath day. Reviewing the events of his Presidential years, he could not have failed to see fruition and triumph written on them. The broad Republican coalition of Northern merchants, farmers, and industrialists had succeeded in changing the balance of power. He himself spoke for that coalition. Under him, middle-class liberalism was the dominant new force in American life. The man surrendering in Appomattox that day, Robert E. Lee, represented the planter aristocracy. Not only an army, but a way of life, was finished.

In addition to carrying on the war, Lincoln had pushed other policies which pointed to the new day—such measures as the Land Grant College Act, the Homestead Act, the tariffs and the railroad bills. The United States now would quickly become a world power, a leading example of democratic government in the western world.

All this would not be easy. The problem of the defeated South defied calculation. The spirit of rebellion would smolder for years to come. Violence would continue and spread. For every American as magnanimous as Lee or Lincoln, there would be ten filled with vengeance and hatred. The war had been a shattering experience for the North as well as for the South. Northern politicians were bent on seeing Dixie pass under the Caudine Forks, and her leaders swinging from sour apple trees. Southern politicians, on the other hand, would find a major road to power through racism and prejudice. The victory the Southern white had not won from the Yankees he might now wrest from the Negro who was freed, dazed, and walking to the New Jerusalem without a roadmap. The bloody shirt in the North and the bloody fist in the South were to become American symbols.

Lincoln's own program of reconstruction was magnanimous and merciful. Rebels must become Americans again; secession must be forgotten. In terms of actual political and military power, Lincoln, Grant and Sherman towered over the shattered land. All three, and most of the soldiers under them, sought peace at any price, so long as the Union was preserved and slavery abolished. Knowing this, and aware that Congress was not scheduled to meet again until December, Lincoln was confident that his program of reconstruction would prevail.

The main outline was clear in his mind. Southern states should be readmitted to all privileges of the Union as soon as ten per cent of the whites took the oath of allegiance and organized a state government. Instead of keeping the recent enemy under heel, the Federal government would help him to his feet.

The President had summed this up neatly when he gave General Weitzel his instructions for administering conquered Richmond: "If I were in your place, I'd let 'em up easy; let 'em up easy."

Dusk was settling over the sluggish Potomac. The little *River Queen* came within sight of Washington. Standing at the rail, the Presidential party gazed at the irregular skyline, dominated by the large-domed, still incompleted Capitol.

"That city is filled with our enemies," said the sharp-tongued Mrs. Lincoln.

"Enemies—we must never speak of that," her husband replied quietly.

The ship docked. A carriage was on hand to take the Lincolns back to the White House through a city exploding with jubilation. At four-thirty that afternoon, while Lincoln was moving up the river, General Grant had telegraphed Secretary of War Stanton: "General Lee surrendered the Army of Northern Virginia this afternoon on terms proposed by myself. The accompanying additional correspondence will show the conditions fully."

As soon as this was known the people erupted in what Noah Brooks wryly called "exclusive jollification." Four years of pent up emotion and frustration exploded with that one announcement. There was screaming, shouting, parading, drinking, exalting, swearing. Men embraced, shook hands, tooted horns, broke windows, kissed their own wives, kissed anybody's wives, rode horses backwards, rang churchbells, got drunk, and tried to defy the law of gravity. The Dance of Death was over, and people danced for joy. Lee's surrender, for so long a wild dream, was now at last a wonderful reality.

"The news is from Heaven," wrote James Russell Lowell. "I wanted to laugh and I wanted to cry, and ended by holding my peace and feeling devoutly thankful." On that frantic, hilarious, abandoned day, when women prayed in the streets and the *Te Deum* rang from the churches of the land, some were too moved to shout. "I sat dumfounded for an hour," Edwin L. Godkin admitted.

Lincoln did not return to his city like a newly acclaimed Caesar. Indeed, he did not join the revelers at all. Instead he made his way quickly to the bedside of his painfully injured Secretary of State, William Seward. On April 5, Seward had been thrown from his carriage by runaway horses, picked up unconscious on the street and treated for a dislocated shoulder, broken jaw, and painfully bruised body. Entering his gaslit room and sitting quietly at his side, Lincoln saw the pained, swollen face of his faithful friend looking out at him through a steel frame.

"You're back from Richmond?" Seward managed to say.

"Yes," Lincoln replied, and tried to convey what he had seen and done there. But Seward soon fell into a feverish slumber, so his visitor tiptoed from the room. Back Lincoln went into the world full of sound and laughter; down the muddy streets, past the riotous crowds, back to the White House, teeming with visitors and plotters. Having greeted those whom he could not avoid, he fell into his bed to sleep.

Others did not sleep. They celebrated. When the sun arose the next morning, people had already gathered in Lafayette Square in front of the White House. The number increased by the minute. At breakfast Lincoln was serenaded by a well-liquored rendition of "The Star-Spangled Banner." Across the way in the Treasury Building and—in fact—throughout the Union, men were gathering to sing "Old One Hundredth"—"Praise God from whom all blessings flow."

Thinking as always of his family, the President sat down that morning to scribble a note to the Secretary of War which read: "Tad wants some flags. Can he be accommodated?" The lad already had a captured Confederate flag which, to the crowd's delight, he waved from the White House window.

Realizing that they had come to see him too, Lincoln walked out on the balcony on the second floor, above the main entrance facing Lafayette Square. A wave of sound sharp as buckshot greeted him and subsided only when he held up his hands to indicate that he would speak.

He congratulated the crowd on the victory, and said arrangements were under way for a formal occasion at which he would speak.

"We can't wait!" a happy, boisterous voice yelled.

"I will have nothing to say later if you dribble it out of me now," Lincoln went on in the same light vein. Then, to divert his audience to something else, he added, "I see you have a band."

"We have *three* of them!"

"Well, I'll close by requesting you to play a certain piece of music—'Dixie,' one of the best tunes I ever heard."

This little quip had worked well on the band that gathered when he left Virginia two days earlier. Lincoln was shrewd enough to use it again at what could have been an embarrassing moment for him and a disappointing one for the merry makers. "Our adversaries over the way tried to appropriate it. I insisted yesterday that we had fairly captured it. The Attorney General gave the opinion that it is our lawful prize. I ask the band to give us a good turn upon it."

They did, and then played "Yankee Doodle" as a counterpart. By then, the President had disappeared into the Presidential mansion.

All day long people milled around the White House. Lincoln tried to appease them by sending out messages, but that did not satisfy the crowd. They wanted to gaze at Father Abraham, to listen to what he thought, and to hear him make up a little story that illustrated his point. They had come to realize that his ideas moved in pairs, like the animals in Noah's ark; and they wanted to be able to tell their children and grandchildren what the Great Emancipator said that day.

In the afternoon he came on the balcony again. Finally they stopped shouting and let him speak. "Persons have been gathered here at different times during the day, and in the exuberance of their feeling, called upon me to say something. I have, from time to time, been sending out what I suppose was proper to disperse them for the present . . . I would prefer having this demonstration take place tomorrow evening, as I would then be much better prepared to say what I have to say."

Faces in the crowd showed their disappointment. Where was the Lincoln touch? The President anticipated the unspoken question and went on to say, "Everything I say, you know, goes into print." The faces were smiling again. "Thank you for the compliment of the call. I bid you good evening."

A journalist, who was standing near the President, wrote of the episode for the editor of *Harper's Monthly*. "Lincoln appeared somewhat younger and more off hand than I should have expected," he reported. "His bright, knowing, somewhat humorous look reminded me of a well-practiced country physician who had read men through until he understood them well. He was happy, and glad to see others happy."

Lincoln moved away from the large mob outside the White House to the smaller one inside, one which could change his office into a wailing wall or a chamber of special pleading at any hour of day or night. That day, too, the outer rooms teemed with people. Among those who were admitted were two women from Pennsylvania come to ask clemency for men who had avoided the draft. Lincoln requested a list of those held and said, "I believe I will turn out the whole flock." In a moment the release paper was signed, and the older lady was kneeling before her benefactor.

"Get up, don't kneel to me," said Lincoln, echoing his words to the Richmond Negroes who had so honored him the week before. "Thank God and go."

His old confidant and friend, Joshua Speed, watched the pair of visitors. "It's a wonder such scenes as this don't kill you," he said.

"I ought not to undergo what I so often do," Lincoln admitted. "I am very unwell now. My feet and hands of late seem to be always cold, and I ought perhaps to be in bed. But what you just saw doesn't hurt me. That scene is the only thing today that has made me forget my condition or given me any pleasure. I've made two people happy and alleviated the distress of poor souls whom I never expect to see. Speed, die when I may, I want it said of me by those who knew me best, that I always plucked a thistle and planted a flower when I thought a flower would grow."

Most of the next day, April 11, the Chief Executive devoted to writing the speech to be given that evening. He signed several proclamations, including one to close all Southern ports, thus stopping the profits of blockade-runners. Then in the afternoon, he went to the War Office to catch up on the latest telegraph reports. He took time to tell a story to Charles Tinker, the telegraph operator, then hurried back to his busy office. After supper, Lincoln watched a light mist gather over Washington, then put the final touches on what would be the last major speech of his life.

He made it from the White House balcony. At first, he

held a candle in his left hand, the speech in his right. When this proved difficult, he let his aide, Noah Brooks, hold the candle.

"Fellow citizens," Lincoln began, "we meet this evening not in sorrow, but in gladness of heart." Having congratulated those who won the fight, he warned how difficult it would be to win the peace. "We simply must begin with and mold from disorganized and discordant elements." Then he continued with a carefully written account of recent policy, especially in regard to the state of Louisiana. "What has been said of Louisiana will apply to other states," he went on. "Yet so great peculiarities pertain to each state, that no exclusive and inflexible plan can be prescribed." It might be his duty, Lincoln concluded, to make some new announcement to the people of the South. "I am considering this, and shall not fail to act when satisfied that action will be proper."

Too long and too carefully reasoned for the fiesta-minded crowd, the speech was not well reported or reviewed. The New York *Tribune* thought it "caused a great disappointment and left a painful impression." "The President was so afraid of misconstruction or criticism that he said nothing, or what comes so near to nothing that he might as well have not broken silence at all," said the New York *World*. "Mr. Lincoln gropes, in his speech, like a traveler in an unknown country without a map."

Already alarmed by the President's clemency, Senator Charles Sumner quickly condemned the speech. "This and other things augur confusion and uncertainty in the future, with hot controversy," he wrote.

Just how Lincoln might have handled Sumner and those who wrecked the program he began to reveal during the week after Palm Sunday, we shall never know. That he intended to go ahead with his plans, oblivious of Congressional criticism, is certain.

But now, the inevitable greetings and handshaking completed, President Lincoln retired to his bedroom and was soon asleep. He would need all the strength he could muster in the difficult days ahead.

As Lincoln turned to his duties on the morning of April 12, Robert E. Lee was beginning his journey back to Richmond. That gutted and destroyed city was in chaos. Lincoln sent a long telegram to General Weitzel who already was in troubled waters. The same morning, the President had a lengthy memorandum from Chief Justice Chase on constitutional issues raised by his remarks about Louisiana. With every hour, the problems mounted. Nothing would make Lincoln change his mind about general principles, however, or about the rule of thumb which he had stated for Weitzel in Richmond. He was still going to "let 'em up easy."

The peace and equanimity he craved for others seldom came to Lincoln. In addition to the incessant opposition of men around him, Lincoln himself also had to endure the conflicts created within his own mind. Throughout his life he was fascinated by dreams and omens. Toward its close, this interest became almost an obsession. On Thursday, April 12, Lincoln told his wife and several guests of a dream so portentous that it has won a special place in the American saga.

"About ten days ago, retiring very late, I soon began to dream," the weary leader said. "Then I heard subdued sobs, as if a number of people were weeping. I thought I left my bed and wandered downstairs. There the silence was broken by the same pitiful sobbing, but the mourners were invisible. It was light in all the rooms. Every object was familiar to me. I was puzzled and alarmed. What could be the meaning of this? In the East Room I met with a sickening surprise. Before me was a catafalque, on which rested a corpse wrapped in funeral vestments. Soldiers were acting as guards. 'Who is dead in the White House?' I demanded of one of the soldiers.

" 'The President,' he answered. 'He was killed by an assassin!' Then came a loud burst of grief from the crowd which awoke me from my dream." Grave, gloomy, and pale, Lincoln was nevertheless perfectly calm as he recounted this dream.

"I wish you had not told it," Mrs. Lincoln said.

"Well, let it go. I think the Lord in His own good way and time will work this out all right."

While Lincoln was contemplating death in Washington, his Confederate counterpart, Jefferson Davis, was speaking of survival. On April 11 he had written General Johnston that the big question was "at what point concentration shall be made, in view of the present position of the two columns of the enemy." And when the last Confederate high-level conference was held the next day, Davis still spoke of defiance.

"My views are, sir, that our people are tired of the war, feel themselves whipped and will not fight," Johnston said bluntly.

"I think we can whip the enemy yet, if our people will turn out," Davis insisted. But to his wife back in Richmond, he wrote: "Everything is dark. You should prepare for the worst ... I have lingered on the road and labored to little purpose."

The White House docket for Good Friday was heavy. Though a deeply religious person, President Lincoln did not consider it a holiday. As on most other days, he expected to arise early, tend to office business until eight o'clock, have breakfast and return for morning visitors. The Cabinet was to meet at eleven. After lunch more conferences, trips to the War Department, meeting with friends, a late afternoon ride with Mrs. Lincoln. The most unusual engagement was for an evening at the theater. Lincoln was not enthusiastic about this. *Our American Cousin,* a third-rate social satire, was playing. Since Mrs. Lincoln insisted, her husband had not objected to going. He realized he needed a little relaxation.

On that Good Friday morning, he sat for a photograph in the studio of Alexander Gardner. Few American photographs have been so much studied, so often reproduced. It is the only time in his Presidency that Lincoln permitted a broad smile to wreathe his face. The joyful look does not, however, hide the signs of the terrible days through which he had just passed. He was thirty pounds underweight, his cheeks were hollow and haggard, and his eyes sat back in unfathomable black sockets.

As he sat before the lens, he may well have been thinking of another picture, one his son Robert had brought him at the breakfast table that morning—one of Robert E. Lee. After putting it on the table to study carefully, Lincoln had said: "It is a good face. I am glad the war is over at last."

Good Friday was in fact hectic for both Lee and Lincoln. The former was going to the home of his brother Carter in

Tidewater for those family greetings and tears soon to become the daily routine of Southerners. Lincoln was meeting with his many-faceted Cabinet; the victorious General Grant was a special guest. The President praised Grant and his men warmly. He insisted that there was to be no persecution now that Lee had surrendered. As he talked on, sitting by a south window, the subject of dreams once more asserted itself. On the preceding night he had seen an indescribable vessel moving swiftly towards an indefinite shore. The others listened without comment.

Then Grant gave a full account of the events at Appomattox. "What terms did you make for the common soldiers?" Lincoln asked.

"I told them to go back to their homes and families, and they would not be molested if they did nothing more," the General replied. The answer pleased Lincoln. Many other problems were discussed in the two-hour meeting. No sour note was struck at this moment of triumph. Lincoln asked that they come together again on April 18 to continue their deliberations.

That afternoon, however, Lincoln's mood changed suddenly to one of concern and gloom. Speaking to his faithful bodyguard, he said: "Crook, do you know, I believe there are men who want to take my life?"

"I hope you are mistaken, Mr. President."

"We cannot prevent what Fate decrees," Lincoln said. He went on to mention his engagement to visit the Ford Theater that evening. "It has been advertised that we will be there, and I cannot disappoint the people. Otherwise I would not go."

On that cold raw night the Lincolns left the White House, their home for four years and forty-one days. They drove in their carriage along Tenth Street, between E and F Streets, to the Ford Theater. Arriving about nine o'clock, they went right to the Presidential box where they would have a good view of the stage and could follow the silly puns and the contrived humor of the play. Neither the President nor anyone in his party noticed that a small hole had been bored in the door to his box so that someone could peer through from the outside. Nor did they notice that, close to the door connecting with the balcony, two inches of plaster had been carefully cut away so that a wooden bar could be inserted to block anyone's entry. No one inside the box suspected that John F. Parker, who was supposed to guard the door, would wander off and leave it unguarded. The well-set trap was about to be sprung.

The course of American history was changed by a lead ball, about half an inch in diameter, which crashed into the back of Lincoln's head three inches from the left ear, moved obliquely forward toward the right eye, and lodged a few inches behind that eye.

At twenty-two minutes past seven on the morning of April 15—the day Robert E. Lee entered Richmond—Abraham Lincoln made his exit from the world. Nothing could be done now, except to mourn, and be numb, and carry the Railsplitter back across the nation he had loved and preserved.

III

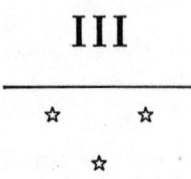

THE PHOTOGRAPH

> Laden with countless woes and desolations,
> The life-blood freezing round a broken heart.
> —Paul Hamilton Hayne

FOR FOUR YEARS Robert E. Lee had faced Yankee guns. Now he had to face a Yankee lens. Having spent his life doing what he ought to do, he would do this, too. "We are ready, sir," he said to the photographer. "Where do you want us to stand?"

April 17, 1865—Richmond, Virginia—General Lee, his son Fitzhugh, and his aide, Colonel Walter Taylor, posed for a bushy-haired beak-nosed Union photographer named Matthew Brady.

The Confederate chieftain was not pleased, and he showed it. He was wound up as tight as a watch on which the main spring might snap at any moment. Like the Confederacy, which had gone thundering down in ruins in days just past, Lee was stunned and dazed. On occasion, time moves too fast for the human mind and heart to absorb all that has happened. This was just such an occasion.

April 17, 1865. The corpse of the Confederate States of America was ready for interment. A few years earlier, the fiery secessionist, Robert Barnwell Rhett, had dreamed of the day when the Confederacy would stretch to the Pacific "and down through Mexico to the other side of the Gulf, and over the isles of the sea." That dream, all it entailed, and all that depended on it, were to be buried. In retrospect, it would fascinate Poet Stephen Vincent Benet:

> And with these things, bury the purple dream
> Of the America we have not been,
> The tropic empire, seeking the warm sun,
> The last foray of aristocracy . . .
> The pastoral rebellion of the Earth
> Against machines, against the Age of Steam.

Because the society Robert E. Lee fought for has been submerged and buried so completely, it is hard to realize how he must have felt when he had to attend the South's funeral.

A fine photograph is frozen history. Peering at one Brady made on that April morning almost a century ago, we can see for ourselves what sort of a figure Lee was: well proportioned, strong knit, erect, with beautifully formed features, small feet, and expressive hands. Just under six feet tall, he weighed about one hundred and seventy pounds. His large head (in circumference, twenty-three and one-half inches) was marked by brown eyes, prominent brows, wide temples, and sat on a strong neck. His narrow hips supported a massive torso, so that he looked larger than he actually was. Agile and graceful, he was often likened to Apollo by those who saw him in action.

He had none of the small vices—smoking, drinking, chewing, swearing—and his enemies seldom accused him of the greater ones. A meticulous man, Lee had taken care to don for Brady his best uniform, the one he wore confronting Grant at Appomattox. Olympian and aristocratic, he looks out with a boldness and certainty that is unspeakably grand. While the classical beauty in this face has been touched by tragedy, no look of reproach or despair mars it. A chapter of terrible agony had just been closed; a hint of that agony is mirrored in Lee's eyes.

His son and his aide also show the strain. They are still somehow at war. These are men who have been forced to play God—to take human life and mete out final judgments. Massive strength still hovers around them. So does an intense devotion and attachment to the leader of the Army of Northern Virginia. Here was a man who was weathered as an oak tree is weathered. But defeated? Never.

Brady worked rapidly and skillfully, realizing that this was a great hour both for him and for American photography. At forty-two, he was not only an artist and war veteran, but also an historian of note. He had risked his life many times to document the struggle.

After news of the surrender reached him in Petersburg, he rushed to Appomattox, only to find the cupboard bare when he arrived. Souvenir hunters had bought or stolen every object in the room where the surrender papers were signed. Quickly Brady followed Lee to Richmond, hoping to photograph him there. Appearing at Lee's door on Franklin Street, he presented his request, but was refused politely. General Lee was in no mood for photographs. Undaunted,

Matthew Brady pleaded both with Mrs. Lee and his old friend Robert Ould, a Confederate official. These two in turn spoke to the General, who reluctantly agreed to give Brady an hour on the basement porch in the rear of the house.

After necessary but minimum civilities, Brady got on with his business. He had known Lee since the Mexican War, but he sensed that this was no time to reminisce about the past. "There was little conversation during the sitting, but the General changed his position whenever I wished him to," Brady later wrote. Lee, the good soldier, made a good subject. But he left no written record or recorded comment on this, his most famous photograph. We can only peer at the defiant aging eagle, and wonder about what he did and did not comprehend on that April morning a century ago.

Certainly he must have sensed that in the future "those people," as he called his Northern adversaries, were determined to push aside "his people" with their aristocratic prerogatives and privileges. Despite his determination to stay out of politics both during and after the war, Lee could see the handwriting on the wall as plain as anyone, and plainer than most. Inflated phrases and promises, be they Confederate or Union, never impressed him. He could be slyly sarcastic about those who talked while he fought. In peace, as in war, Robert E. Lee was a realist. The man who had said that the Rebel soldier's one unswerving friend was the lowly goober pea wasn't apt to expect much from Reconstruction politics.

He understood that, in addition to the sharp odor of gunpowder, there was definitely the sweet smell of profits in the balmy spring air. Lincoln's Secretary of the Treasury, visiting New York earlier that spring, had noted that many people there paid more attention to the stock market than to the casualty reports. To this a New York editor added: "Real or professed patriotism may be made to cover a multitude of sins. Gallantry in battle may be regarded as a substitute for all the duties of the Decalogue."

This comment was as true in the South as in the North. Romantic Southern legends do not feature the blockade-runners, black marketeers and draft dodgers; but they were very much on the scene. In the Northern states, the rapid transformation from a conglomeration of farmers to a nation of industrialists had been hastened by the war. The exclusion of the Southern planters from the halls of government made the change considerably easier. Astronomical profits on wartime speculation and gouging encouraged rapid expansion. While brave boys in Blue and Gray shed blood on the battlefields, the crafty made profits back home. The nation which Lee confronted on April 17, 1865, was demoralized —the South by defeat, the North by victory.

Eleven states were out of the Union, at the mercy of a not too merciful Congress. The Southern economy was smashed. Refugees, white and black, wandered over the land. Four million Negro slaves heard they were free, but hardly knew what the words meant. Their former masters wandered about in a wilderness of crumbling walls, naked chimneys and dead trees. Dixie was a howling waste.

No king or prince can stay Death's icy hand or his sharp sickle. The shattered Union, without a president on either side of the battle line once Davis had abdicated and Lincoln was assassinated, reached its psychological nadir the week Lee returned to Richmond. Thieves, deserters and looters roamed the land. Hymn books, communion service and even bells disappeared from churches. The battles were over, but death had not been sated.

Men whose names have been lost to history—like Lieutenant Albert Davidson of Giles County, Virginia—still had to pay with their lives. Only twenty-three, he was murdered by a group of ruffians as he was trying to protect a woman. "We knew him well," a local paper said, in the only public notice Davidson received. "He was a young man of great worth and promise, an efficient officer, who left behind a wife and a two-weeks-old child. Now all the Davidson boys have been killed in the war. Well may we exclaim with the poet: 'Insatiate Archer, would not one suffice?' "

For weeks, clerks in the War Office would be tabulating the deathly toll. At least 360,000 Union men were killed, and 260,000 Confederates. What of the maimed, mutilated, crushed and crazed? No one could say. What of the mental pain that continued after the physical pain was cured? No one could measure it. No one ever will.

A dazed nation looked to Washington for leadership. On April 15, in an atmosphere of confusion and woe, Andrew Johnson was sworn in as the Chief Executive. A fierce Unionist, North Carolinian, former owner of eight slaves, he was not anti-Southern. Commanding wide bipartisan support, at first he was hailed as a "firm" man who could be expected to alter policies of the "lenient" Lincoln. But lacking both Lincoln's judgment and his compassion, Johnson soon proved to be unsuited for the difficult role of Chief Executive.

On April 17, General Mosby surrendered his army to Yankee General Hancock at Berryville, Virginia. The following day, Johnston yielded to Sherman in North Carolina, bringing effective Southern resistance to an end.

Caught up in an orgy of hysteria and remorse and guided by Stanton, the vindictive Secretary of War, the North had already launched the "great man hunt" the day Lee kept his appointment with Brady in Richmond. For a week, John Wilkes Booth was the quarry. Once he and his accomplice, Herold, were captured at the Garrett farm beyond the Rappahannock, attention shifted to the fleeing Jefferson Davis. A one-hundred-thousand-dollar reward was placed on his head. But not until he was taken at a camp in southern Georgia on May 10 did President Johnson announce to the world: "Armed resistance to the authority of the United States may be regarded as at an end."

If the drama of collapse and surrender centered in the South, the drama of growth and expansion focused on the West. Hundreds of millions of dollars would go there; the receding frontier would be whittled down by systematic attacks of the Yankee investor. The Federal government would help by showering the railroads and settlers with land and services. Mines, cattle and farming would boom. Where bayonet had never been, the dollar would invade and conquer.

Robert E. Lee neither comprehended nor understood this kind of invasion. Full of courage and military genius, he suffered nonetheless from myopia. Although he had lived and struggled in the trans-Mississippi West, he seldom thought about it during or after the war. While the South was his constant concern, he did not usually mean the Confederacy when he spoke of "my country." He meant the Commonwealth of Virginia.

That technological and social revolutions were going on in 1865 was completely beyond Lee's ken and interest. For a few years, he was a key figure in American history. Remove him from the conflict any time after 1863, and you change the whole picture of the war. In the world after Appomattox, the world of McCormick reapers, Otis elevators and Pullman sleeping cars, Lee was more of an outsider than a participant. He had neither inclination nor ability to join the new order of things.

In the spring of 1865, Lee's war was over, but the Indians were on the warpath. The heroic day of the cowboy, cavalryman and sod buster was beginning. The whole middle frontier was afire. When emigrant trains were captured, men were roasted over a spit, castrated or subjected to the slow shaving away of all body flesh. Women were raped incessantly, suffering unspeakable pain. It was the last great round between primitivism and civilization for the possession of a continent.

The Bozeman Trail was opening, moving out from the Platte River in Colorado to Virginia City, Montana, cutting through the last unspoiled Indian hunting ground. The Plains Indians would make newcomers pay dearly for every foot of ground. The same General Custer who lorded over the Confederates at Appomattox would be brought low in the bloody West. In American folklore, the Man in Gray would give way to the Man with the Sombrero. Significantly, the cowboy novel that set the pattern for half a century would be called *The Virginian*. Lee's thoughts, however, did not turn to the West but to the desecrated and spoiled Virginia fields. . . .

His work completed, Matthew Brady thanked General Lee who bowed stiffly and went back inside the house. He would not find there the silence and privacy he craved; instead, the bravado and adulation he despised. For days, an unending stream of people would make a pilgrimage to 707

East Franklin Street—soldiers, statesmen, politicians, ministers, wives, mothers, widows, journalists, artists. In vain would Lee's family and friends try to protect him from visitors. Too many of them had good reason to come and could not be turned aside by polite excuses. In April of 1865 the whole South revolved around this house and the man in it. Defeat imposed its own special obligations, more demanding than those of victory. Now Lee had to give himself to those who had given their all to him.

Members of his family noted the change in attitude and appearance that came over him once he assumed the role of private citizen. "He looked older, more quiet, and reserved," his son Robert wrote. "He seemed very tired, and was always glad to talk of any other subject than that of the war." There was no other subject, at that moment, either for the old warrior or his loyal admirers. It had consumed them like a fire. How could they speak of less significant things, except as a device to hide what was in their hearts? Time alone would heal the open wounds. At this particular moment, there was more hurting than healing.

Lee leaned heavily on his wife now, as he had done in all his other crises. She was not much support. She never adjusted either to the rigors of war or the finality of defeat. Poor health made her a hopeless cripple. Much of Lee's early life had been spent nursing an invalid mother; his last years would center around an invalid wife. Her courage and her husband's cheerful acceptance of his obligations are impressive and memorable features of their marriage.

Vainly did the General's son Robert and cousin Dan try to turn away insistent visitors. All sorts of people came. There was, for example, a rugged battle-hardened Union sergeant, Irish all over, who appeared at 707 East Franklin

Street, accompanied by a Negro carrying a basket full of food.

"I've come to see me old Colonel," he announced. "He'll know me from the days with the Second Cavalry. They tell me he's without food, and I've brought some." Then, without further to-do, he came right into the house.

Hearing the conversation, Lee went out into the hall. The leather-faced sergeant drew himself up erectly, saluted, said, "Colonel, Sir—" and burst into tears. General Lee shook his hand, told him they were not wanting for food, and asked him to leave it at the hospital where men were in dire need. With tears streaming down his cheeks, the Irishman threw his arms around Lee as he left and said, "Goodbye, Colonel! God bless ye! If I could have got over in time, I would have been with ye!"

Not long afterwards two worn, emaciated Confederate foot-soldiers appeared. They wanted to take their General west with them to the mountains where they could stand off the Yankees forever. Lee explained that he couldn't go. This time his own eyes filled—eyes that had been clear and dry a week earlier at Appomattox.

To control himself now was a more demanding task than that he had faced week after week on the fields of battle. To oppose advancing cavalrymen is one thing; to look at a weeping mother whose son has been killed is another. Bear in mind that Lee was not only a professional soldier. He was also an eminent Victorian, raised in an age of sentimentality and chivalry, whose taste in poetry ran to such works as Sir Walter Scott's *Lady of the Lake*. Remarkably dispassionate towards his own sons, he melted before any words or requests of his daughters. Undoubtedly that first week in Richmond after Appomattox was a greater strain on Lee than any single week of the War between the States had been.

Some soldiers still came to him as to their commanding general. Young Channing Smith, courier for Mosby's unsurrendered Rangers, slipped in under cover of darkness to ask him for instructions. Lee explained that he himself was on parole and could give no military advice. Later on, Smith wrote: "What a change in General Lee's appearance! The last time I had seen him, he was in the fullest glory of his splendid manhood, and now he is pale and wan with the sorrow of blighted hopes. I could not help nor was I ashamed of the tears which filled my eyes."

As we have already seen, not all those who came to pay homage to Lee of Virginia had worn the gray. Union General George Meade appeared, urging Lee to take the oath of allegiance and to set an example of acquiescence. Lee was grateful for such sincere advice, especially when it came from a soldier he respected as much as Meade. He promised to do all he could to promote peace. Not all who came dared to advise, or even converse. A badly wounded Texas veteran merely wanted to shake Lee's hand before beginning his long walk home. When the General extended his hand, the man sobbed, covered his face with his good arm and rushed away. Neither man spoke a single word.

If Matthew Brady photographed only the pale shadow of the leader Channing Smith had followed in battle, it is hard to imagine how magnificent the Lee of battle must have been. Mild-mannered in the drawing room, he was a tiger on the field. His claws could bring red spurts of blood on the green landscape. Under the controlled classic façade was incredible strength. Lee recognized this latent power, and spent a lifetime trying to use it wisely. "It is a good thing that war is so terrible," he was heard to say as his forces won a major victory at Fredericksburg, "else we would love it too much."

Of his intimate feelings and hopes between Fredericksburg and Appomattox we know little. Lee was a self-contained man. His final official report of April 20 to President Davis has a poignant simplicity. "I see no prospect of achieving independence. It is for your Excellency to decide, should you agree with me in my opinion, what is proper to be done."

That month Lee did not merely lose his army. He lost his position, his property, and his profession as well. But he did not lose his faith nor the admiration of many who had fought both with and against him. Offers for employment would reach him from business houses, insurance companies and railroads. An English lord made available a manor house befitting one of Lee's station. Politicians sounded him out for offices of high trust and power. None of these propositions interested or tempted Robert E. Lee. He had a mandate for simple usefulness. He was a good soldier. He would just do whatever he had to do.

IV

THE LETTER

> The pen
> Turns to the waiting page, the sword
> Bows to the rust that cankers, and the silence.
> —Donald Davidson

THE WELL-PLANNED LIFE of Robert E. Lee was frequently shaped by the unpredictable and accidental. A casual remark by his daughter in the summer of 1865 was the catalyst that brought about a chain reaction which shaped the pattern of Lee's last years. She made the remark to a Richmond lady.

"The Southern people are willing and ready to give Father everything he needs—except the chance of earning a living for himself and his family," she said, with the tart touch that was Mary's hallmark. The comment was passed on to Colonel Bolivar Christian. He thought it was his duty to report Miss Mary's comment to the Washington College trustees when they met in August to nominate a new college president.

"Are you nominating the General?" a fellow trustee asked.

"No," Colonel Christian replied quickly, "I merely wanted this group to know what Miss Lee said."

After that, no other names suggested seemed of consequence. If General Lee would actually come to the little valley college, and if—

After repeated urging, Colonel Christian *did* nominate General Lee. All other names were withdrawn. The roll was called, and Lee was unanimously elected.

Stunned by their own boldness, the trustees sat staring at one another for a moment. General Lee as the head of an almost defunct and bankrupt college tucked between the Blue Ridge and the Alleghenies? What were they thinking about?

"Some one must notify him," the Rector said. It was like the gathering of mice elated over the vote to tie a bell around the cat's neck—until someone asked who would approach the cat.

As is often the case, the man who raised the question won the assignment. "You should go, Judge Brockenbrough," Colonel Christian said. The Judge quickly declined, pointing out that his clothes were too shabby and he could not afford new ones.

"I've just received a suit from a son in the North," Hugh Barclay said. "I'll loan it to you for the occasion." Thus one problem was solved. How to transport the impecunious Judge to Tidewater, since neither he nor the college had funds? This was more difficult. Finally the name of a local lady who had just been paid for a tobacco crop was mentioned. Perhaps she would loan them funds with such a trip in mind. She did. Clad in his borrowed suit, the college

Rector used his borrowed money to travel to Tidewater, and ask General Lee to accept the presidency of Washington College.

The man whom he visited was going through one of the most difficult periods of his life. "We must be resigned to necessity," he had told a cousin in Richmond, "and commit ourselves in adversity to the will of a merciful God." This was easier to say than to do. Harassed by constant visitors, saddened by failure, embarrassed by having to live as a charity in another man's home, unable to expend his energies in any constructive enterprise, Lee made no secret of his desire to move. "I am looking for some quiet little house in the woods," he wrote to General Long in May, 1865. "I wish to get Mrs. Lee out of Richmond as soon as practicable." Lee rode frequently into the countryside, both to find privacy and to search for the "little house" that would never be his.

Meanwhile the demoralization and corruption of the times distressed him. So did comments in the Northern press, such as this statement by Indiana's George W. Julian: "I would hang Jefferson Davis in the name of God. What an outrage that Lee is unmolested too. I would hang liberally while I had my hand in. I would give the land to the Negroes and not leave a rebel enough to bury his carcass in."

Thundered William Lloyd Garrison: "I know that in the South the powers of hell are still strong and defiant, resolved upon doing whatever evil is possible in a spirit of diabolical malignity."

These tongue lashings hurt the South almost as much as the physical destruction of earlier months. They made an honorable return to free and independent Union all but impossible.

Radical Republicans, free now of Lincoln's restraining hand, traded his New Testament mercy for Old Testament vengeance. Thaddeus Stevens was their leader. His long face, beetling eyebrows and protruding underlip seemed to imply that he lived to pronounce Dixie's doomsday. He would take an eye for every one given, until, like Oedipus, the blinded protagonist dwelled in endless deserved darkness. Incorruptible as Robespierre, he was equally incapable of compassion. His counterpart in the Senate, Charles Sumner, put the proposition simply: the rebel states had committed suicide. They were territories, subject to the exclusive jurisdiction of Congress; conquered provinces, to be given the heel. The proud nobility should be stripped of property, the aristocracy annihilated. The mighty should be laid low.

The furrow-faced President Lincoln, who had spoken from the White House portico on the very day Lee entered Richmond after Appomattox, had said: "Whether the Southerners have ever been out of the Union does not concern me. Finding themselves safely at home, it would be utterly immaterial whether they had ever been abroad." Those words were forgotten now.

A bad situation was made worse by the defiant action of Confederate President Jefferson Davis. Stubbornly refusing to concede defeat, he escaped and headed south. In North Carolina, he urged General Joseph E. Johnston to continue the futile struggle. Johnston refused, and on April 18—the morning after Brady photographed Lee in Richmond—he surrendered his little band to General Sherman. But the implacable Davis fled on, insisting that his government would triumph even after the last Confederate forces east of the Mississippi surrendered on May 4. Six days later, however, Davis was captured near Irwinsville, Georgia. Shortly afterward, General Kirby Smith surrendered the trans-Mississippi forces. On June 22, the C.S.S. *Shenandoah*, pride of the Southern Navy, fired her last shot. On July 4, General Joe Shelby and his Irreconcilables sank their Confederate battle flags in the Rio Grande and exiled themselves to Mexico. It was all over.

In the months immediately following, Lee could not ignore the marked change in Southern temperament: the decay of hospitality and the growth of hostility. The war had not merely been a time of physical destruction, but of social revolution. Life in America, to quote Walt Whitman, became "canker'd, crude, superstitious, and rotten." A raw and unlovely decade followed the heroic war years; an age caught in painful transition. Knowing that he could not make the change, Lee decided to represent the *ancien regime* as a citizen, just the way he had done as a soldier. Many things could be taken from him, but not his honor.

So, instead of trying to rebuild an industrial and commercial Richmond, he rode off to visit the plantations where "his people" still lived. One frequent stop was Pampatike, the home of his cousin, Thomas Carter. While here, he learned of President Andrew Johnson's May 29 Proclamation. This document stated the terms of amnesty and pardon for Southern rebels. Lee was in a category which had to make special applications for pardon on an individual basis. To this group Johnson promised "such clemency as may be consistent with the facts of the case and the peace and dignity of the United States."

Thus the door was opened for a settlement of old grievances. Lee did not hesitate to walk through it. Back in Richmond, he wrote President Johnson this letter:

June 13, 1865

Sir: Being excluded from the provisions of the amnesty and pardon contained in the proclamation of the 29th, I hereby apply for the benefits and full restoration of all rights and privileges extended to those included in its terms. I graduated at the Military Academy at West Point in June, 1829; resigned from the United States Army, April, 1861; was a general in the Confederate Army, and included in the surrender of the Army of Northern Virginia, April 9, 1865. I have the honor to be, very respectfully,

Your obedient servant,
R. E. Lee

Four days later he wrote to his devoted aide, Colonel Walter Taylor, who had told him of the misery and discontent of many Confederate veterans. "Tell them they must all set to work," Lee replied, "and if they cannot do what they prefer, do what they can. Virginia wants all their aid, all their support, and the presence of all her sons to sustain and recuperate her."

This reference to Virginia, as well as scores of others throughout Lee's life, suggests one of the keys for understanding him. Lee and Virginia were inseparable; beyond her borders, his vision became astigmatic. "When I speak of my country," John Randolph had said when Lee was a young man, "I mean the Commonwealth of Virginia." So did Robert E. Lee.

The major task of Lee's life was not to split the Union or defeat the Yankees, but to preserve traditional Virginia society. In a family-centered world, his was the first family, the genealogical center of a proud and flourishing society. That it was built on chattel slavery—a moral and political evil which Lee condemned—was one of history's ironies. That one of America's best military minds was absorbed in defending an institutional pattern which Virginia's best political minds had long declared indefensible was one of history's tragedies.

Whatever years of Lee's life we study, we find identical patterns of thinking. One concerned Virginia. As a regular army officer torn between remaining with the Union or joining the Confederacy, he reduced the issue to a single lucid proposition. "If Virginia stands by the old Union, so will I," he said. "If she secedes (though I do not believe in secession as a Constitutional right, nor that there is sufficient cause for revolution), then I will still follow my native state with my sword and, if need be, with my life." Nothing that happened during or after the Civil War changed this feeling toward his native state.

There is no logic, and questionable wisdom, in such blind loyalty. That it existed is a fact which anyone who tries to understand Robert E. Lee must accept. Lee's heart and heritage wedded him to Virginia. Divorce was out of the question. If there is narrowness here, there is power too—as with the narrow stream that carves gaps in solid granite.

In 1865, Lee's Virginia was sullen and somber. Even when summer came, the psychological mood was autumnal. Brown was the pervasive color: the brown of scorched earth, dead trees, renounced ambition and once-green hopes. Dead men were everywhere. Their portraits covered parlor walls. Their death masks filled public places. Their words echoed in speeches and sermons. They seemed to be concealed in the widows' weeds. The tempo of their lives echoed in the pounding of comrades' wooden legs on cobblestones. Soon they would ascend to marble blocks and guard dozens of courthouse squares.

To many Virginians, defeat and disgrace were almost unbearable. Lee's gallant aide and courier, John S. Wise, drew up his own mock will:

"I, J. Reb., being of unsound mind and bitter memory, and aware that I am dead, do declare the following to be my political last will and testament . . . I direct that all my shares in the venture of secession shall be canceled, provided I am released from my unpaid subscription to the stock of said enterprise. My interest in the civil government of the Confederacy I bequeath to any freak museum that may hereafter be established. And now, being dead, having experienced a death to Confederate ideas, I depart . . ."

Equally bitter was Inness Randolph, an ex-major in General Stuart's cavalry and member of one of Virginia's leading families. He summed up his attitude in a poem which enjoyed a wide vogue:

> Three hundred thousand Yankees
> Are stiff in Southern dust;
> We got three hundred thousand
> Before they conquered us;
> They died of Southern fever,
> And Southern steel and shot,
> I wish it was three million
> Instead of what we got!
>
> I can't take up my musket
> And fight 'em any more;
> But I'm not going to love 'em,
> Now that is certain sure.

> And I don't want no pardon
> For what I was or am;
> I won't be reconstructed
> And I don't give a damn.

General Jubal Early, having gone first to Mexico and then to Canada, sponsored an emigration of ex-Confederates to New Zealand; Matthew Fontaine Maury planned an exodus to Mexico; Judah P. Benjamin escaped to England where he became Queen's Counsel. Other high Confederate officials followed him to Europe. Some imitated the most dramatic exit of all, that of Edmund Ruffin. On hearing of the defeat, he wrapped a Confederate flag around his body and blew his brains out.

The spirit of the times was expressed in Southern groups like the Ku Klux Klan, the White League, Knights of the White Camelia and Order of the White Rose—all racist and terrorist in nature. In their literature hysteria and hyperbole were mixed: *"Dies Irae!* The wolf is on his walk—the serpent coils to strike. Action, action, action! By Midnight and the Tomb; by Sword and Torch and the Sacred Oath, the Clansmen will greet you at the newmade grave."

Against the words implicit and the acts implied by such groups, Robert E. Lee, soldier-turned-citizen, fought constantly in the closing years of his life.

Deciding what to do with the Washington College offer, once Judge Brockenbrough had appeared at his door and made it, was another kind of struggle for Lee. Earlier he had turned down the vice-chancellorship of the University of the South and a job inquiry from the University of Virginia. The first was church, the second state, controlled. Lee did not feel he was in a position to join either faculty.

That Washington College was independent of both church and state put it in a different category.

Lee had not pictured himself as finding employment on a campus but on a farm where he might enjoy "no end of cream, fresh butter, and fried chicken—not one fried chicken, or two, but unlimited fried chicken." Should he go, instead, to a war-ravaged school with four teachers and forty students, an institution as nearly dead as it could be, without being abandoned altogether?

Usually decisive, Lee could not decide. A letter from his old chief of artillery, Brigadier General W. N. Pendleton, now Rector of Lexington's Grace Episcopal Church, encouraged but did not fully convince him. Lee sought the advice of another Episcopal minister, Joseph B. P. Wilmer of Albemarle County. Riding west on Traveller, he laid the matter before Wilmer, who was at first cool to the proposal.

"The institution was one of local interest and comparatively unknown," Wilmer said later. "I named others more conspicuous which would welcome him with ardour as their presiding head." Lee explained that this was not a matter of prestige or reputation. The cause gave dignity to the offer. This door, and not another, had been opened to him by Providence. If he could do the job and through it help the South, he would accept.

To anyone as family-conscious as Lee, earlier Lee connections with the college must also have carried weight. William Graham, a close friend of his father, had once directed the school which grew into Washington College. Light Horse Harry Lee sent his third son, Henry, to study there; he was a student at the college when Robert E. Lee was born in 1807. Moreover, Robert's sister, Anne, later married William Marshall, another president of Washington College. Nor should the magnetism of the name "Washington" be forgotten when speculating about Lee's affirmative decision.

The letter of acceptance was actually penned in Powhatan County on August 24, 1865. Unlike his somewhat brittle military reports, it was graciously wrought. With the exception of his April 20, 1861, letter resigning from the United States Army, this was the most important document of his life. No single letter holds such a decisive spot in Lee's post-Civil War story.

"Gentlemen," wrote Lee, "I have delayed for some days replying to your letter of the 5th inst., informing me of my election by the board of trustees to the presidency of Washington College from a desire to give the subject due consideration. Fully impressed with the responsibilities of the office, I have feared that I should be unable to discharge its duties to the satisfaction of the trustees or to the benefit of the country. The proper education of youth requires not only great ability, but I fear more strength than I now possess, for I do not feel able to undergo the labour of conducting classes in regular courses of instruction. I could not, therefore, undertake more than the general administration and supervision of the institution.

"There is another subject which has caused me serious reflection, and is, I think, worthy of the consideration of the board. Being excluded from the terms of amnesty in the proclamation of the President of the United States, of the 29th of May last, and an object of censure to a portion of the country, I have thought it probable that my occupation of the position of president might draw upon the college a feeling of hostility; and I should, therefore, cause injury to an institution which it would be my highest desire to advance.

"I think it is the duty of every citizen, in the present condition of the country, to do all in his power to aid in the restoration of peace and harmony, and in no way to oppose the policy of the State or general government directed to that object. It is particularly incumbent on those charged with the instruction of the young to set them an example of submission to authority, and I could not consent to be the cause of animadversion upon the college. Should you, however, take a different view, and think that my services in the position tendered to me by the board will be advantageous to the college and country, I will yield to your judgment and accept it; otherwise I most respectfully decline the office. Begging you to express to the trustees of the college my heartfelt gratitude for the honour conferred upon me, and requesting you to accept my cordial thanks for the kind manner in which you have communicated their decision, I am, gentlemen, with great respect, your most obedient servant,

R. E. Lee"

Behind the letter is the image of a humble man, anxious to save others from chagrin because of his presence, wearied by watching day and night the moves of numberless enemies, and realizing that the eyes of a shattered Confederacy centered on him. The letter was also a tangible proof that he believed the South's hope lay with her young, not her old; and that the time for military maneuver and civil insurrection was irrevocably past. The attitude which lay behind it was not one of passive acceptance, but of optimistic acquiescence to the very changes he and his men had fought desperately to prevent. Lee sided with hopeful programs, not lost causes. Southern independence, as the Confederate leaders had conceived it, was not to be. The job now was to find and foster better causes.

The August 24 letter, written with hesitancy, was received with joy. The Board of Trustees was elated with Lee's reply. Meeting in Lexington on August 31, they "heartily concurred and fully indorsed the sentiments so well expressed by Gen. Lee in his letter of acceptance." So far as assuming office was concerned, they urged him to do this as soon as possible. Lee might not have many years left. If he were to make a mark in peace, as he had already done in war, there was no time to lose.

With young enthusiasm, Lee began his last and most difficult campaign. He spoke of "a self-imposed task which I must accomplish. I have led the young men of the South in battle; I have seen many of them die in the field; I shall devote my remaining energies to training young men to do their duty in life."

Plainly, Lee was not suited by training or interest for an academic post. To the intellectual and scientific battles which shook the nineteenth century, he had given little or no thought. Even in his special field, military science, he had not been a diligent reader for years. Unlike Stonewall Jackson, Lee had not spent hours poring over the campaigns of Caesar, Frederick the Great or Napoleon. Later on, appearing before a Congressional committee, Lee admitted that he "scarcely ever read a paper." Yet he agreed to become ruler of a tiny paper kingdom because he thought it was the most significant testimony he could make at that moment in history. On September 15, he left Tidewater and headed toward the Blue Ridge Mountains. Less than a month after he had mailed his August 24 letter, he himself set out for Washington College on his charger, Traveller. The road from Richmond to Lexington was only one hundred and eight miles long; but at the end of it he would find a new life and struggle.

When the man of war becomes a man of peace, where are the new battlegrounds? That is what Lee must have asked himself as he headed west toward the mountains. He wore no sword and no medals now and his major campaigns had not yet even opened. The Wilderness, Antietam, Gettysburg and Petersburg lay behind him. Ahead was the ancient Blue Ridge—and green hopes for a new life.

V

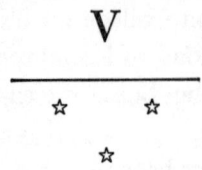

THE VALLEY

> I see clear waters run in Virginia's Valley
> And in the house the weeping of young women
> Rises no more.
> —Donald Davidson

THE PATH THROUGH Rockfish Gap winds like a giant cork-screw up from the rolling Albemarle County meadows, over the Blue Ridge Mountains, and back down into the Shenandoah Valley. Ever since colonial days travelers taking it have enjoyed the godlike view from the summit of Afton Mountain. On a crisp fall day in 1865 a lonely figure on horseback moved slowly up the trail.

At Mountain House, an inn on the Albemarle side of the ridge, he asked about quarters for the night. A young lad and a colored servant told him there was room. Nodding, the gray-haired traveler led his horse to the stall and watched the servant remove the saddle. A raw spot on the animal's shoulder caught their attention.

"I know a cure for that, mister," the boy said. "Moss

from the chalybeate spring down by the gate." Nodding again, the guest led his horse by the halter to the spring. Plunging his arm and hand into the clear cold water, the lad plucked up a handful of dark green moss and held it, dripping, for the rider to apply carefully to the mount's sore.

"Thank you. What is your name, young man?"

"Jimmie Minor."

"Thank you, Jimmie. Don't you want to ride back to the stable?"

"Oh, yes, sir!"

Grabbing the boy by the seat of the trousers, the man hoisted him on the horse's back. As they approached the inn, the bugle voice of a hound dog cut through the air. "Donder must have found a rabbit, or maybe a fox," the boy observed.

"We can tell in a minute," the man said. "If it's a fox, the cry will be continuous; if it's a rabbit, it will be interrupted."

After a few intermittent yelps: "Guess it's a rabbit!" Jimmie said. "Wish I was out with him."

The man smiled and walked into the plain country inn. Jimmie went over to the rack where the servant Uncle Mose had placed the saddle.

"Sure is a nice man," Jimmie said. "Just look at the leather in this saddle." As he ran his hands over it, his eyes rested on a small brass plate with the owner's initials: R. E. L.

General Lee was too tired to walk about and listen to Donder's baying. This was his third day on the road. Both man and beast were glad to rest before starting the last lap of their journey. Leaving the Tidewater plantation, Derwent, early on September 15, Lee had reached Bremo, the home of John Hartwell Cocke in Fluvanna County in the early afternoon, and had spent the night there. A long, hard ride the next day had taken him to the Reverend Joseph Wilmer's home, five miles north of Scottsville. These first two days Lee described as "very hot." Since Wilmer's advice had been instrumental in Lee's going to Washington College, the Episcopal minister was pleased to house him en route to the new job.

Reaching Rockfish Gap now about three o'clock on the afternoon of September 17, Lee decided to get a good rest before moving down into Rockbridge County and the hamlet of Lexington which was to be his new home. He wanted to absorb the cool mountain air and the Olympian vista to the west.

Shenandoah Valley—Daughter of the Stars in the Indian tongue. Here the Great Spirit brought the stars together once every thousand years. Angels came, too. On the spot where a chief angel stood, a spring of water gushed forth. At every place where an angel's tear fell, there sprang up flowers to fill the valley with fragrance. So thought the Cherokee, Catawba and Susquehannock Indians who hunted here. Rimmed by mountains, the valley abounded with slim, bending elms, plump, sweet maples and gnarled many-fingered oaks. Green pines pierced the horizon. Buffalo grass was higher than a hunter's head. Paradise must be something like this.

John Lederer, the first white man to write of the valley, did not, like Lee, come from the east but from the north. Arriving in 1669, he killed rattlesnakes and wolves and watched a wildcat slaughter a deer. The next year Lederer was bitten by a spider and returned to the seacoast.

Other pioneers followed him, to live with the wail of wolves and whippoorwills. Their journeys were significant, but they were not spectacular like that of Governor Alexander Spotswood who came in 1716 with his Knights of the Golden Horseshoe. The well-lubricated cavalier determined to call the slow-moving river the Euphrates. Those who arrived later preferred the more modest name Shenandoah.

"I have always inclined to favor those who came to settle on the western side of our mountains," Governor William Gooch wrote in 1739, when incoming Presbyterians petitioned him for permission to build a meeting house. "No interruptions shall come if you conform to the rules prescribed."

With this encouragement, sturdy Scots came: the McClungs, McCorkles, McCormicks, McCulloughs, McDowells, Mores, Paxtons, Leyburns and Robinsons. They were still there when Robert E. Lee arrived in 1865. Their stone churches dotted the landscape, and their stern sermons filled the Sabbath air. To a Tidewater aristocrat like Lee, accustomed to gentlemanly manor houses and ways, the change must not have been entirely to his liking. But he knew he had to get used to the valley, and he intended to do just that. If he could never fully understand the Presbyterians, he would at least take care never to offend them.

Behind him, on the eastern side of the Blue Ridge, was the zone of the Book of Common Prayer. This was Calvin's country, where sermons occupied most of Sunday's daylight hours and where the administration of the Lord's Supper went from Friday to Sunday. He wasn't the first Episcopalian to feel separated from his own sort of people. Young George Washington had surveyed this land for Lord Fairfax in 1748, and had noted in his diary that the settlers he met "seem to be as Ignorant a Set of People as the Indians." Living conditions were not ideal. One of the beds the lad had slept on was "nothing but a little straw matted together without sheets or anything else, but one threadbare blanket with double its weight of vermin such as lice, fleas, etc."

In 1767, a youthful colonial named Thomas Jefferson was so anxious to see the "natural bridge" he had purchased for twenty shillings that he did not worry much about bedding when he came over from Charlottesville. He followed the same route that Lee took a century later. During the Revolution, Hessian officers, sent to the valley as prisoners of war by General George Washington, found little there to please their aristocratic taste. "We do not have good neighbors here," one of them wrote. "There is hardly a *Gentleman* living within Forty miles of Staunton."

Gentlemanly Robert E. Lee, who was to live well within forty miles of Staunton, made no such complaint. His adjustment to the valley people and environment was quick. This particular phase of his career and thinking has been slighted by Lee's biographers. They have stressed the Cavalier inheritance and plantation environment on his youth, but not the Calvinistic inheritance and small farm environment which shaped his final years. In the less pretentious and mannered west where a vein of iron ran through the people and the land, Lee made some of his most important judgments and decisions. The character of the valley was a major factor in his last years.

Down from Afton Mountain the General rode, on a clear fall morning, past the hamlet that later became the city of Waynesboro. Ahead were little villages hovering round a church spire or clinging lichenlike to the mountain slopes. Throughout the day he saw mill wheels crushing mountain torrents into a million sparkling jewels, turning the valley wheat into flour. He passed the graves of men who had died fighting Indians when the valley was on the cutting edge of the frontier. Near Fairfield he might have noted a typical marker:

> HIER LYES THE BODY OF
> JOHN MACK DOWELL
> DECD DECEMBER 1743

Closer to the General, in time and impact, were Civil War memories. Along the roads he now traveled, Confederate General Jubal Early had been routed less than a year ago by Yankee General Phil Sheridan. Although Lee did not pass through the town of New Market, he knew how the Virginia Military Institute cadet corps—"seedcorn of the Confederacy"—in their early teens met and repulsed the Yankees there, winning immortality.

Many times during the war Lee had counted on men and supplies from this area. His greatest lieutenant, Stonewall Jackson, famed for major victories here, was now resting in the town toward which Lee was going. We shall never know what part this played in Lee's choosing Lexington, or how much he thought of Jackson on this trip. So much of Lee's story will never be known.

But no one could hide the scars of the recent struggle. "The whole country from the Blue Ridge to the North Mountain has been made untenable for a rebel army," Sheridan had informed Washington. If a crow wanted to fly across the area, he would have to carry rations. Trees were down. Fields were gutted. Fences, mills, barns, bridges, crops and stock had been destroyed. Instead of wheat, corn, and barley, the fields were overrun with briars, nettles and weeds. The fields could be improved in a season; the people's tempers and bitterness not for generations. Sectional antagonism went back far before the war. "We do not set any claims to public spirit in the matter of internal improvement," a Rockbridge County historian admitted as early as 1852, "and are shamefully content to let all the glory that appertains there go to the go-ahead Yankees." When the Yankees went ahead and laid waste to the Shenandoah Valley, Virginians turned from sarcasm to denunciation. Against this all-consuming hate Lee had to fight after he came to Rockbridge in 1865.

People did not quickly forget the fate of towns like Scottsville, where every shop, mill and store was burned. Canal locks were dismantled. Records and books were wantonly scattered. The little town lay in its blackened pall, a returning soldier wrote "like a mourner hopelessly weeping." If the small towns were bad, the cities were worse. The closest major city to Lexington was Lynchburg, a transportation and manufacturing center fifty-four miles to the southeast. In 1865, life there was paralyzed. Stores were vacant. The tobacco business was ruined. Property everywhere declined in value. The occupying soldiers were a rowdy, rough and drunken set. Robberies occurred nightly. No wonder families in the region memorized and recited Bishop Beverley Tucker's poem:

> Though the battle may be over,
> Yet its horrors still remain;
> Though the cannon's voice is silent
> Still we hear the clanking chain.
> And the graves of sleeping heroes
> And the exile's lonely hours
> Warn us that the days of pleasure
> But resemble faded flowers.

Down through desecrated Augusta County and into Rockbridge County, Lee rode, passing through Greenville, Steele's Tavern and Fairfield. He saw the once-green fields in which Cyrus McCormick had invented the reaper, thus furnishing the Union with a major factor in the Northern war effort. Lee entered Rockbridge County near the spot where Benjamin Borden, who held the first land title in this area, crossed in 1737. After Borden, came thousands of settlers, headed for Kentucky, Tennessee and North Carolina. Never in remembered history had the valley looked so desolate and barren as in 1865.

But the men would get to work and make it produce again. Hard labor was part of their heritage. Their ancestors had made a living from animal skins, flax and hemp. After that, tin and timber were marketed. Iron had been extracted ever since 1779, when Daniel Dougherty built his forge on Irish Creek. Ironmongers like John Jordan and William Weaver put a dozen furnaces in operation; the Bath Iron Works was making thirty tons of pig iron a week by 1835. With fourteen thousand inhabitants, Rockbridge County was in that year one of the more wealthy and promising Virginia counties. Since the North River, which drained the county, tied in with the James, it was accessible when the canal boom came. The county seat of Lexington was described by an English visitor as "surrounded by beauty, standing at the head of a valley flowing with milk and honey." At the same time, it had none of the sophistication and style of Tidewater. "Families here have little social intercourse, except occasional visits and marriage feasts," the Englishman reported. "Nothing is known of the gay amusements common among the lower Virginians."

Place names which Lee heard en route to his new home reflected the honest, literal, earthy men who had first settled there: House Mountain, Hogback Mountain, Thunder Peak, Tinkling Spring, Timber Ridge, Mossy Creek, Purgatory Creek. Like so many Nehemiahs, the first Rockbridge County men had built God's houses with one hand, and in the other hand held the weapons to destroy the ungodly enemy. The grimness of the eighteenth century had spilled over into the nineteenth.

The Episcopal Church, of which Lee and his family were members, had never flourished here. The Calvinists, who fought the Established Church at home, gave it no quarter abroad. For generations they recalled ancestors' tales of the persecution of Claverhouse and the cruelties of Dundee. Stone Presbyterian meeting houses dotted the valley before the Revolution. Not until 1843 did a tiny Episcopal church appear in Lexington. Ten years later the Reverend William Pendleton came as rector. The meager salary tendered him was six hundred dollars a year. When a smallpox epidemic swept the area in 1859, all the regular places of worship were closed except for Pendleton's church. His approach to life must have been different from that of his Calvinist neighbors. Here is the advice he gave his young daughter when she went away to school: "Laugh, run, skip about, amuse yourself just as much as you can, in all the time allowed for it. See how much enjoyment you can get and give. Remember, I regard it as not a whit more your duty to acquire Latin, French, etc., than it is to improve in strength, weight, and color."

The fact that Mr. Pendleton, a West Point graduate and then a Southern general, was in the rectory now was one of the reasons Robert E. Lee, his companion in many a battle, rode toward Lexington in September, 1865.

Rockbridge County had favored the Whig Party ever

since Andrew Jackson's opponents established it in the 1830's. Unlike the Jeffersonians on the other side of the Blue Ridge, the valley people did not take a cosmopolitan pro-French view. Instead, they favored a protective tariff, internal improvements, and a United States Bank. Feeling little sympathy with the aristocratic planters to the east—the Lees, Carters, Byrds and Randolphs—valley politicians had been opposed to early talk of secession and the extension of slavery in the west. Prominent citizens like Samuel McDowell Reid, James Davidson and Samuel Moore backed the Constitutional Union Party. They were far more in sympathy with their neighbors to the west in what became West Virginia than they were with their Tidewater neighbors east of the Blue Ridge.

The Rockbridge County vote in the 1860 elections made this clear. Bell, the Constitutional Union candidate, polled 1,314 votes to 630 for Douglas and 352 for Breckenridge. A Rockbridge County man, John Letcher, occupied the Governor's Mansion in the troubled days of that election. He did much to keep Virginia in the Union after her sister states to the south had formally seceded. Once Virginia herself was invaded, however, Union sentiment disappeared in the valley. And after the Union raids, it became a stronghold of resentment against everything Yankee.

One of Lee's illustrious predecessors as head of Washington College was the ardent Unionist, George Junkin. When a Confederate flag appeared over the Main Hall in 1861, the President promptly removed it. Immediately the students made known their desire "that the Confederate flag continue to float, and we therefore respectfully request that you will not suffer it to be taken down. There can be no opposition to it from any quarter now, except from the enemies of Virginia." Finally matters became so tense that President Junkin had to get a carriage and dash northward to safety. When he crossed the Potomac, he carefully wiped all the Virginia dust from his horses' feet to show his unwillingness to carry any southern sentiments with him.

The action of Letcher, Junkin and other valley notables makes us appreciate more the old Scotch-Irish prayer which began: "Oh Lord, set my feet in the right path, since Thou knowest I am not easily changed."

On toward Lexington Lee rode, delighted with distant mountains veiled in delicate blue, green grass pushing up through the debris, glossy patches of mandrake, purple patches of violets and the floating shadows of high thin clouds. Not like *his* Virginia, this was beautiful and inspiring in its own right. In whatever time was left to him, he would know and love the valley.

The Great Path down which Lee traveled that day had been used by buffalo, Indians and countless settlers before him. First they had walked, then brought their ox-carts, covered wagons and stage-coaches. Part of the road was built of planks, laid crossways, as a device to keep the wagons out of the mud. Rumbling along with their cargoes of beeswax, tallow, feathers or human beings, they were the key to this inland empire beyond the mountains.

Mighty good men had been born along the path. The house of one, Sam Houston, was a landmark near the Timber Ridge church. Lee must have seen it as he neared Lexington. Closer to town was the birthplace of Big Foot Wallace, and on down the road, that of Stephen Austin. Having served in Texas himself, Lee knew something of its early history. It is hard to imagine what that saga would have been without the boys from Rockbridge.

THE VALLEY

Lee studied the terrain, the houses and the fields that he passed that day. Later on he would talk of them and mention them in his letters. On Traveller, he would ride all over the county and enjoy the landscape again and again. Whatever nostalgia he felt for the life that was behind him was carefully concealed. Everyone who talked with Lee after 1865 agreed that he seemed very much at home in the new environment.

Because he had been close to his men in the Army of Northern Virginia, Lee already knew much about how the valley people thought and talked. Though they had no slaves, the mountaineers fought with a devotion and courage that made them infantrymen second to none. Their folklore and speech was archaic and beautiful. They told how, because the robin plucked a thorn from Jesus' temple, the robin's breast is red. They knew that the rust spots on dogwood leaves came from the nails of His Cross. To cure the "achin's," they put a spider in an old quilt and hung it around their neck. By their campfires, they reflected aspects of past ages which they did not themselves always understand:

King Arthur was turned into a raven. In the springtime he likes to circle over the Shenandoah Valley. Raven once snow-white, became a tattle tale, now he is black. If you see a wolf before he sees you, you'll drop dead. If a white pigeon settles on your chimney and an owl screeches at noon, danger is near. A lone appletree is not just a tree in springtime, but a bride adorned for her husband . . .

These people, soon to be Lee's neighbors, brought him their lore and their food: walnuts, chinquapins, squirrels and venison. There was something tender and lovely in this relationship.

Thus the ex-general who entered Lexington in 1865 was not going to his exile. No evidence can be found to support Donald Davidson's contention that Lee spent his last years:

> Listening long for voices that never will speak
> Again; hearing the hoofbeats come and go and fade
> Without a stop, without a brown hand lifting
> The tent-flap, or a bugle call at dawn,
> Or ever on the long white road the flag
> Of Jackson's quick brigades. I am alone,
> Trapped, consenting, taken at last in mountains.

Lee was *released*, not *taken*, in Virginia's mountains. There he could spend his days among the living, not the dying. There he could find a meaning in nature that never emerged in politics, and achieve an inner resignation which was more impressive, in perspective, than all the victories he and Jackson ever won. All this must have been in Lee's mind when he said, near the end of his days, that the greatest mistake he ever made was becoming a soldier. Such a statement, coming from one of the most talented field officers in American history, is the best single epitaph for Lee after the Civil War.

VI

THE TOWN

> The town is like a place distressed
> and forsaken.
> —Samuel Pepys

SIXTEEN MONTHS BEFORE General Lee came to Lexington alone, General David Hunter had come—with an army. His orders were to subsist on the country, to destroy all supplies and burn all houses within five miles of the spot where resistance occurred. Defeating a small Confederate force near Port Republic on June 6, 1864, Hunter took Staunton and headed for Lexington with 18,000 Federal troops. Bombarding the town from across the North River, he crossed on a pontoon bridge, burned the Virginia Military Institute, and looted the area.

Annie Broun echoed the natives' reaction in the helpless undefended town: "Can I say 'God forgive him'? Were it possible for human lips to raise his name heavenward, angels would thrust the foul thing back again. The curses of thousands will follow him through all time, and brand upon the name Hunter infamy, infamy."

Arriving on September 18, 1865, Lee could still see for himself what had been done. Atop the bluff near the river stood the charred and blackened ruins of the "West Point of the South"—Virginia Military Institute. Along the streets were piles of rubble and brick. At the edge of town stood Washington College, desecrated and silent. Once-white columns were chipped and crumbling. Planks were nailed over smashed windows. Obscenities were scribbled on the walls. Part of the campus was under cultivation. Lee did not stop to examine the College closely. He continued up the muddy hill that was Main Street to the hotel in which he intended to spend the night.

To one from eastern Virginia, familiar with Alexandria, Williamsburg and Georgetown, Lexington was not an old town. Staked out of what had been Isaac Campbell's farm, its charter was dated May 14, 1778. In 1796 a devastating fire destroyed most of the houses. The state legislature in Richmond authorized a lottery to rebuild the frontier town, with streets named for Virginia's patriots: Washington, Jefferson, Henry, Randolph, and Nelson. By the administration of Andrew Jackson, the little town began to expand and prosper.

Older than Lexington was the educational institution which Lee had come to direct. Augusta Academy was opened between Staunton and Lexington in 1749. Robert Alexander, an Edinburgh University graduate, directed this one-room schoolhouse, the first classical academy west of the Blue Ridge. As a patriotic gesture, the name was changed to Liberty Hall in 1776. By then the principal was William Graham, a man "passionately fond of froliking and dancing, whenever he had the opportunity." Under him, Liberty Hall acquired two hundred and ninety books, a telescope, quadrant, globe and a "very small orrery." Graham had Liberty Hall Academy incorporated by the Virginia legislature in 1782. In 1793, a stone building was erected at the cost of two hundred pounds. Here Mr. Graham labored until his resignation in 1796.

The school named Liberty Hall Academy did not shower freedom on its pupils. Early in the morning the day was opened with prayers. After that every student was expected to apply himself silently and diligently to his tasks, and not to go out without permission "until dismissed with prayer in the evening." Monitors on duty noted and reported any violations of the rules. The rod was not spared and the pupils were not spoiled. If the school's aspirations were high, costs were low. Food for a whole session cost twenty-three dollars and seventy-five cents in 1795. Room rent was half a dollar.

George Washington made a generous gift of canal stock to the Academy. The grateful recipients changed their name to Washington Academy in 1798 and to Washington College in 1813. Shortly afterward, a major building program was undertaken on a ridge overlooking Lexington. The Washington College group, erected in the 1820's, was the nucleus of the institution to which Lee came.

That a sound and rigid curriculum flourished there before the Civil War was heartening. President Archibald Alexander was a firm believer in the classics, holding that the ancient languages "are an important branch of liberal education which cannot, without great injury, be laid aside. The opinion which is hostile to the study of Latin and Greek as a part of liberal education, mistakes the primary object of education." In 1859, there were ninety-five students at the College, all but one of them from Virginia.

The small town boasted a second educational landmark. Founded in 1839, the Virginia Military Institute was famous in ante-bellum days. One of the guiding spirits was the Frenchman Claude Crozet, a soldier under Napoleon, who wore the Cross of the Legion of Honor. First Professor of Mathematics at West Point, he helped develop the V.M.I. studies along the same lines. For half a century, the Institute was supervised by General Francis H. Smith who became one of Lee's closest friends in Lexington.

For years the two institutions had coordinated part of their work and schedules. From 1839 to 1847, for example, the College and the Institute held joint commencements in the Presbyterian Church. But the College had labored to attain independence both from the Presbyterians who dominated the area, and the state government which controlled V.M.I. In this the ante-bellum college presidents were successful. Financial and intellectual freedom was one of the most important inducements which caused Lee to accept the presidency.

Arriving one day earlier than planned, Lee intended to rest quietly before meeting the college officials. This was not to be. As he prepared to dismount in front of the Central Hotel, several veterans saw him and rushed over. A moment later, Professor James J. White, who happened to pass by, recognized Lee. Introducing himself, he insisted that Lee go straight to Colonel Reid's house. Lee agreed with some hesitation. He did not want to impose. The two men continued down Nelson Street, and Lee was graciously received at his host's home.

The full extent of the town's disruption became clear to

Lee in the days following. The money system had largely broken down. Barter was the order of the day. A pound of sugar was worth a pound of butter, a dozen eggs or a chicken. Tradesmen worked for money or produce of any kind. Many people were in debt, with no prospect of getting out of it. The editor of the local newspaper, the Lexington *Gazette*, reported that Dr. R. L. Madison expected to leave the county, adding tartly that if those who owed him would pay up promptly, he might be induced to remain. That printers were having as much trouble as everyone else finding hard cash was plain from a prominently displayed list of "Special Imprecations on the Man Who Won't Pay the Printer":

> May 543 nightmares trot races over his stomach every night—
>
> May his friend run off with his wife, and his children take the whooping cough—
>
> May his cow give sour milk, and may he churn rancid butter—
>
> May his daughter marry a one-eyed editor, his business go to ruin, and he to—the Legislature!

A few days before Lee reached Lexington, the *Gazette* had carried a notice indicating what problems would attend restoring the now-defunct college. "A large number of valuable books have been carried off from the libraries of Washington College, some honestly and some dishonestly, within the last two or three years. That model Librarian, John W. Fuller, Esq., will take the greatest pleasure in receiving the missing books or in going after them." Other local people were facing hardships with courage and determination. Underneath the notice was an advertisement by the coach builder, William A. Rhodes. "My books were burnt, ink spilt, and goods destroyed. William is left to himself again. Now I am a citizen of the U.S.A., but not under the same system of credit as in older days. Old Carriages and all kinds of country produce taken in exchange for work."

The happiest announcement in the September 13 issue had appeared under the heading WASHINGTON COLLEGE: "A recent letter from General Lee to Judge Brockenbrough states that he will be in Lexington on the 20th ins., to attend a meeting of the Board of Trustees to be held on that day." Details were given on the repair of the college buildings which were to be ready for the opening of the session on October 3: Terms: tuition $50—all other charges, including room rent, $25. The Board also inserted an ad in the same paper which read:

> 50,000 jointed shingles
> Wanted Immediately at
> Washington College.

Seeing this and other indications of resurging hope, Lee wrote immediately to his family back in Tidewater, assuring them that all was going well. "I have not yet visited the College grounds," he wrote to his wife the day after he arrived. "The buildings are undergoing repairs. The house assigned to us has been rented, and I do not know when it will be vacated." After a closer look at the situation, he realized that overwhelming difficulties confronted the town and the College. "There is no lumber here on hand," he wrote. "Everything has to be prepared. We shall have to be patient."

The Lees might be patient, but not the trustees. On September 20, they convened and appointed a committee to escort Lee to their meeting. Undaunted by lack of resources, they instructed the Treasurer to pay General Lee half of his fifteen hundred dollar annual salary—though it was not due until January. Short on greenbacks, they had plenty of faith.

A public campaign to collect funds was launched at the same meeting. "One of the leading objects of the additional endowment is to secure, beyond contingency, an ample salary to our distinguished President," Judge Brockenbrough reported in the local press. He also announced that the inauguration of President Lee would take place in the near future.

The townspeople were as enthusiastic about the newcomer as the college officials were. Many of the ex-Confederates, especially those from the nearby hills, were still in a fighting mood. They would not hesitate to follow "Marse" Robert, if he but gave the word. Their fighting blood had already been aroused by the appearance of Virginia's wartime governor, William "Extra Billy" Smith, who refused to surrender after Appomattox and came to the western part of the state to rally a guerrilla force. A twenty-five thousand dollar Federal reward on his head did not faze the man whose spectacular military career began at the age of sixty-five. With a brace of pistols strapped to his side, he was ready to open fire again.

Writing from Lexington in June, 1865, the Reverend Mr. Pendleton reported that the Yankees were hunting Smith "like a flea in the mountains. Last night 75 men rode up and searched the town for him. We hear they are come to stay. They are encamped in the meadows opposite the

Institute grounds." Pendleton went on to describe the demoralized state of affairs in town during the fall of 1865. "Our people are for the most part disarmed and exposed to insult and attack from the Negroes let loose. Yankee adventurers are appearing among us with money to cheat our people out of their little remaining coin. We have no country, no currency, no law. I feel almost thankful that so many of our beloved have been taken from the evil here."

Neither the defiance of Smith nor the bitterness of Pendleton were reflected in Lee's words or deeds. He wanted to close the door on the past and the loud rebel yells that greeted him in Lexington on September 21 made him decide to slip off to Rockbridge Baths, eleven miles to the northwest, to avoid such displays. There he took the waters and visited with Mrs. Chapman Leigh and Miss Belle Harrison, two relatives from Brandon. (Did Lee ever go anywhere in Virginia without encountering cousins?) Suddenly, away from all his immediate family and aware of the magnitude of his Lexington task, Lee had to muster all his energy and self-control to endure thoughts of the past and fears of the future. "I feel very solitary and miss you dreadfully," he admitted to Mrs. Lee. Next to the days after Gettysburg and the week following Appomattox, this was one of the most difficult times he ever faced.

On September 30, he mounted Traveller and rode along the winding road leading back to Lexington. There he prepared for his inauguration. Some trustees favored a festive atmosphere, complete with speeches, band music and garlanded maidens dressed in white. This, they argued, would draw national attention and support. Lee would have none of it. He felt that the days of fanfare and glory were over.

At nine o'clock on the morning of October 2, the ceremony was held on the second floor of a repaired college building. The Reverend W. S. White, senior minister in the community, prayed. Judge Brockenbrough spoke briefly. Lee stood silently with folded arms. A local justice of the peace administered the traditional and quaint presidential oath: I do swear that I will, to the best of my skill and judgment, faithfully and truly discharge the duties required of me by an act entitled "An act for incorporating the rector and trustees of Liberty Hall Academy," without favor, affection, or partiality.

Lee signed the document. The county clerk took it for recording. Then Judge Brockenbrough handed the keys of the College to the new president. After brief handshakes, Lee excused himself and left. He had made an exact and legal compliance with the requirements: nothing more. Thus did General Lee abdicate from the military role he had played so well. Now he was President Lee, in charge of a barely functioning college.

Four days after the inauguration, he wrote to R. H. Chilton: "I have entered upon the duties of my new office in the hope of being of some service. But I should prefer, as far as my predilections are concerned, to be on a small farm, where I could make my daily bread." Thoughts of an agrarian utopia haunted Lee's mind to the day of his death.

Without secretary, aide or office staff, he had more than enough to do. The session was scheduled to open on the inauguration day, October 2, and fifty students were on hand. "It is supposed that many more will be coming during the month," Lee wrote. "The scarcity of money everywhere embarrasses all proceedings."

Busy though Lee was, he managed to write constantly to his family in Tidewater, often in a lighthearted and sentimental vein. To his "Precious Life"—Mildred, he wrote: "I suppose Robert would not eat Laura Chilton and Don Ella McKay. Still less would he devour his sister Mildred." The sentence becomes much less cannibalistic when one knows these are the names of Mildred's pet chickens which could not make the long trip to Lexington, and would have to be disposed of. In the same letter, her father made a second reference to chickens: "Traveller is my only companion; I may also say my pleasure. The boys are plucking out his tail, and he is presenting the appearance of a plucked chicken."

From the first, Lee sought rest and solitude in the lovely countryside around Lexington. "Nothing could be more beautiful than the mountains now," he wrote his wife the day after his inauguration. The harshness and ugliness of the human predicament made the serenity and beauty of nature even more attractive to him.

Lee quickly built up among his new associates the kind of devotion he had won from his staff in wartime. His silence, as well as his spoken words, improved their morale. Having reported Lee's inauguration with obvious delight, the editor of the *Gazette* wrote about "our Town" in his October 4 issue. With Lee in Lexington, all would go well. By exercising prudence and courage, the town could both recover and advance quickly. Certain items were critically short: housing, building materials, stores and warehouses, currency. "We want more money," wrote the editor, "in order to do more business and pay our taxes. Cannot capitalists here, or north, south, east, or west, be induced to build a bank for Lexington?" Then he told one of the current jokes—about two dollars meeting on Main Street. They were such strangers that their respective owners had to introduce them formally.

The winter of 1865 was the hump the town and College had to surmount to survive. Unfortunately, Lee had taken over so close to the new term that many Southerners would not hear about it soon enough to choose his school. But even with Lee as a magnet, it would be hard to draw from the prostrate South the caliber and number of students the faculty wanted.

In a section as thoroughly crushed as Dixie, education was a luxury that many could not afford or even contemplate. Ante-bellum academies and schools disappeared, both in name and in fact. The Radical insistence on integrating schools impeded progress everywhere and inflamed the racial issue. Only a few high schools of any stature existed in the whole of Dixie, so that colleges could count on little adequate preparation from newcomers.

Schools much larger than Washington College were slower in opening, and were often unable to continue. The University of the South did not commence work until 1868. The University of Alabama tried to reopen in 1865. When only one student appeared, the doors were closed. By 1869, a few dozen students were on hand; but in 1871 the University was suspended again.

The University of South Carolina reopened in 1866, languished for a decade and closed in 1877 for three years. Heroic efforts of the University of North Carolina to survive political pressures were unsuccessful. In 1870 all classes were suspended, causing a disappointed student to write on a blackboard: "Today the University busted and went to hell!"

To save Washington College from a similar fate was Lee's

considerable task. And because he was the living symbol of rebellion to some Northerners, he could expect constant opposition once he began to succeed. "Aren't you ashamed to give Lee the privilege of being a college president?" one ardent Unionist had written to President Johnson. "Satan wouldn't have him to open the door for fresh arrivals!"

"Fresh arrivals" reached Lexington in the fall of 1865, but not as many as enthusiastic supporters claimed. The Lexington newspapers felt called upon to set the record straight, and did so on October 11, 1865: "The impression is said to prevail in some parts of the country that Washington College is filled to its utmost capacity. A hundred to 150 can still find comfortable boarding and lodging. Our exchange may accommodate by copying this statement."

That same issue carried word that Henry Ward Beecher had said he was entirely convinced that every woman of lawful age ought to be allowed to vote. The Lexington paper could not let this pass without comment. "We suspect that Henry has been put up to this by his sister Harriet (of *Uncle Tom* notoriety). She doubtless thinks herself eminently qualified for a seat in the next Congress." The paper was also happy to carry an advertisement for:

THE NEW YORK DAY BOOK

"The White Man's Paper"

In favor of the Constitution as it is,
And the Union as it was.

If editors and politicians in north and south were anxious to keep the cauldron boiling, Lee was not. Never very interested in political issues and determined not to become embroiled in them after 1865, he concentrated on the many local problems and decisions. When the president's house was finally vacated by Dr. Madison, it was found to be, in Lee's own words, in "wretched condition." He and his friends worked desperately to enable his wife and daughters to come up before Christmas.

The actual move would not be easy; Mrs. Lee's illness complicated matters. Either she and the girls would have to take the Chesapeake and Ohio train to Goshen and complete their journel by stagecoach, or take the canal boat up via Lynchburg. The Lees decided on the boat, though it involved moving at four miles an hour during the day and tying up along the canal at night. The meticulous General sent precise instructions to his family. "Don't take the boat that passed Bremo on Saturday," the General advised, "or else you will have to lie at the wharf in Lynchburg all day Sunday."

In Lexington the one-armed cabinet maker, Andrew Varner, worked day and night to complete the necessary furniture. Carpets salvaged from Arlington were brought down and tucked under so as to fit in the much smaller Lexington rooms. Silver which had been buried during the war was dug up and renovated. Finally all was ready.

On December 2, 1865, the Lee family arrived at the wharves in East Lexington. General Lee was on hand to meet the boat. Riding on Traveller, he escorted the carriage the mile and a half to the house. He never looked prouder or happier than he did that morning. A new life in Lexington was no longer merely a problem or a prospect. It was a reality.

VII

THE RITUAL

> The idea of his life was to do his duty, at whatever cost, and to try to help others do theirs.
> —Robert E. Lee, Jr.

DUTY WAS MORE than a principle to Robert E. Lee. It was a ritual. What he believed he acted out, ceremoniously and solemnly, with as much routine as possible. His strenuous insistence on his own acts of duty and obvious pleasure on seeing regularity in others, was developed early in life and followed him to the grave. The man and the ritual were inseparable.

Before moving into his new home or bringing his family up from Tidewater, General Lee had adopted a rigid Lexington routine. Rising early he washed, dressed, and walked to the College. When the chapel service began at seven forty-five, he was invariably in his seat, having already said his private prayers. At eight he went to his office, kept always in impeccable order, and started to work. Having no clerk or secretary, he had to tend to every routine matter, no matter how small or demanding, himself. In addition to correspondence, planning and administering, he supervised all activities on the buildings and grounds, and approved the outlay of any money. On top of this, he visited the classes regularly during recitation periods and oversaw final examinations.

An exact system of faculty reports was instituted and the President was given a grade for every student every week. When the time came for new reports, Lee was invariably ready for them; by then he had disposed of the business of the previous week.

That such acts were ritualistic does not mean that Lee himself was legalistic. He could stretch or even disregard rules if he thought bigger principles were involved. He tried to keep the framework of responsibility simple enough so it could be understood and obeyed by all. When a post-war student turned up in his office, asking for a "copy" of the rules, the President replied: "We have only one rule here —to act like a gentleman at all times."

Lee met the demands of Washington College, as he had met all others of his life, by working with actual, indisputable facts. Abstract phrases and generalities he tended to avoid. His values were as real as the ground he defended; as the blood he had drawn from the enemy's army and shed from his own. His thought was centered, specific and clear. It had a local habitation and a name.

The twig had been bent and the tree formed, long before Lee rode into Lexington. No one can understand his late years without understanding the early ones. For forty of his sixty-three years, Lee was a professional soldier, dealing with blood, brick and ballast. He was an engineer who cleared fields, dammed rivers and repelled armies. By knowing what the young Lee did and thought, you will understand the ritual which the old Lee lived.

At the core of the man, one does not find mystery or enigma but faith. He knew who he was, where he came from, and what he must do. To the big questions of life, his answers did not change; they simply hardened. Such certainty was joined with simplicity and humility. He did not court greatness; it sought him out. Throughout the war, Lee lived like a Spartan. Meat came to his table only twice a week. When extra supplies were captured, they were put aside for hospital use. Excesses of any kind, in any form, repelled him. He did not waste time, supplies or adjectives. Basically he was a stoic. "Lay nothing too much to heart," he wrote. The words would have done credit to his favorite author, Marcus Aurelius. "Desire nothing too eagerly, nor think that all things can be perfectly accomplished according to our own notion."

Chess was his chief wartime recreation. For a board he used a pine slab with squares marked by a knife and blackened with ink. The table was a three-legged object made of pine branches cut from the woods. This was all Lee needed or wanted. Unrivaled among Southern aristocrats, he lived as simply as any commander in history, and indeed as simply as the men under him.

Yet we cannot call Lee democratic. Nothing in his training or thought favored egalitarianism. Born, reared and married in the patrician milieu, he was at home in manor houses like Stratford, Chatham, Shirley and Arlington. Distinctions of place and position were accepted as part of his birthright. As he watched the Union disintegrate and the work of his ancestors torn to bits, he wrote dolefully: "It has been evident for years that the country was doomed to run the full length of democracy."

Say what you will, you cannot make Robert E. Lee "one of the boys." Fellow officers knew him as a kind but aloof person. "His grave, cold dignity of bearing and the prudent reserve of his manners rather chill over-early or over-much intercourse," said Charles Anderson. General Grant thought Lee "an austere man and, I judge, difficult of approach to his subordinates."

Certainly he could be austere and stern, especially where military duty was involved. This was clear long before the Civil War, as his years in the American West made clear. "Having met with Catumseh, a Comanche chief, I hailed him as a friend," Lee wrote. "But I would meet him as an enemy, the first moment he deserved it." And writing to a friend in Savannah about Indian relations, he said: "I am happy to believe that there is no love lost between us. I see more of them than I desire, and when I can be of no service, take little interest in them. Perhaps our Doctor's lancet has only reserved their sick chief Ha-ten-a-see to die by a bullet."

Harsher yet was a comment to Mrs. Lee: "They [the Indians] give a world of trouble to man and horse, and poor creatures they are not worth it." Here we are close to the old frontier dictum that the only good Indian is a dead Indian. Later on, as a Confederate officer, Lee was a fair but strict disciplinarian. He cracked down mercilessly on deserters and malingerers, indicating time and again that he stood by the letter of the law. He expected others to bring to warfare his total dedication.

A story told after the fighting by a Confederate foot soldier illustrates this: "I was jest out of the horspittle and was strollin' around when the scrimmage come. I saw General Lee on a little rise not fur off. I santered closer to him, still feeling mighty weak. When he looked at me I said, 'Pretty warm work over thar, Gen'ral.' He give me a keen look and says he, quiet-like: 'Where do you belong? Where's your regiment?'

" 'I've been laid up, but before that I was in the Twelfth Virginny.'

" 'I can help you,' says he. 'There's your regiment just going into the fight. Hurry up and join it.' And I did what he said, proud as a pigeon!"

When irritated, Lee had a nervous twist or jerk of the neck which all who knew him feared. "No man could see the flush come over that grand forehead and the temple veins swell on occasions and doubt that Lee had the high strong temper of a Washington," wrote Colonel Venable. Longstreet spoke of Lee's "excessive fury of combat." Colonel Taylor, Lee's aide throughout the war, described him as a man of "positive temperament and strong passions —and it is a mistake to suppose him otherwise." Once Lee was so tart that Taylor lost his temper and threw down the paper in his hand. "Colonel Taylor, when I lose my temper, don't you let it make you angry," Lee said calmly, ending the incident as quickly as it had begun.

Occasionally he exploded in front of a subordinate officer. At Chancellorsville, Lee shouted at General Dorsey Pender: "That is the way you young men always do. You allow those people to get away. I tell you what to do, but you can't do it!" When the enemy escaped at Seven Pines, he snapped at General Jubal Early: "Yes, they will get away because I cannot have my orders carried out."

Recollection of certain Northern acts, like the execution

of Orton Williams as a spy, turned Lee's calm white face red. "My blood boils at the thought of that atrocious outrage against every manly and Christian sentiment which the Great God alone is able to forgive," he wrote to Williams' sister. "I cannot trust my pen or tongue to utter my feelings."

Such flare-ups were always followed by remorse. "Why did you permit that man to come to my tent and make me show my temper?" he once asked Colonel Taylor.

Yet jubilation, as well as anger, could cut through the marble facade. "I cannot express the joy I feel at the victory," he wrote to General Beauregard after Bull Run. And to General Johnston: "I almost wept with joy at the glorious victory achieved by our brave troops. The feelings of my heart could hardly be repressed."

Religious conversations frequently aroused Lee's emotions. On several such occasions, his eyes overflowed with tears and his lips quivered. News of Stonewall Jackson's death, and that if his own daughter Annie, unnerved Lee. Still, few people witnessed his grief on such occasions. What men did see, day after day, was the overpowering sense of duty and the appalling respect for authority.

Acquainted with several Lees, Mrs. Mary Chestnut said frankly that she preferred Robert's older brother. "I know Smith Lee well," she wrote. "Can anybody say they know his brother Robert? I doubt it. He looks so cold, quiet, grand." An unwillingness to yield themselves too readily has always been a trait of Virginia's gentlemen generals. Aloofness plagued George Washington long before Lee, and George Marshall many years after him. Like his own idol, Washington, Lee was no jolly back slapper. He knew there was a time to smile, and a time to scowl. To confuse them was cowardice.

"The young men have no fondness for the society of the old general," Lee admitted in a sad little note to his wife written while he was still with the army in the winter of 1864. "He is too heavy and somber for them." Yet his family and all who really knew Lee realized that he was neither heavy nor somber. As a young man, he tumbled into bed with his children and read them stories while they took turns tickling his feet. As a young officer, he filled his letters to Jerome Napoleon Bonaparte with references to Jenny Lind, Washington Irving, Baltimore belles, and a scheming young beauty who "never attends the feasts of the foxes who have lost their tails." Desperately pressed at Petersburg, he dismounted under fire to replace a fallen bird in its nest. Throughout his life, said his daughter Mildred, he was "always wanting something." Just what this "something" was, Lee never said. Certainly it was not wealth, or power, or fame. The "something" was spiritual, not physical. Perhaps it could not be put into words. Obviously he cared little for the lighter pursuits of life. Lee was a soldier. He liked military chores, fares and cares.

Yet with all this, he was still an extremely human person. Just before the encounter at Gettysburg, he wrote Mrs. Lee, not of the rise and fall of governments, but of something much closer to home: "If my pants are done, will you give them to Mr. Thomas, the bearer, who will bring them up tomorrow? If they are not, keep them. I am on my last pair, and very sensitive, fearful of an accident."

Never a man of the people, General Lee made a significant contribution to democracy: the contribution of his example. What he was and did gave to that critical component of any democracy—its minority—a lasting dignity and significance. Without striving consciously to improve American democracy, he actually did so by establishing a working arrangement between the majority that triumphed and the minority that was crushed.

This indirect contribution did not entail one speck of demagoguery. Pomp, parades and display Lee scorned. Above all else, he hated being made an object of public acclaim. No one disliked more than he the role of the people's hero. Lionized, he did not make an ideal idol. "A true man of honor," he wrote, "feels humble himself when he cannot help humbling others."

Never would Robert E. Lee scramble for favor. Twenty-one years after leaving West Point, he was still a captain: yet he would not push his case. "I know how those things are awarded at Washington, and how the President will be besieged by claimants," he said. "I do not wish to be numbered among them." Later on, when a subordinate asked about promotions, Lee replied: "What do you care about rank? I would serve under a corporal if necessary."

Of all those with whom Lee dealt, he was least civil to reporters. "I shall be glad to see you as a friend," he told a New York *Herald* correspondent, "but request that the visit may not be made in your professional capacity." To another visitor, he said coldly: "I derive no pleasure from my interviews with reporters." When the people and press praised him, Lee shrank away. "They make too much fuss over the old rebel," he would say.

Lee really meant it. He was not puffed up. When he returned to Petersburg after the war, admiring veterans tried to take the horses from his carriage and draw it themselves.

"If you do so," Lee told them, "I shall have to get out and help you."

Then, too, some of the guests in his post-war home left their shoes outside the door at night, thinking a servant would clean them. There was no servant, but the boots were invariably polished—Lee polished them himself.

Just as he did not covet army rank and power before the war, he did not seek it during the war. In the early days of the struggle, instead of being in the center of things, he was on the periphery—in the western mountains of Virginia. His efforts in that theater brought censure, criticism and the nickname of "Granny" Lee. Through it all he stood silent, neither defending himself nor allowing others to do so.

An accident, however, thrust him into a critical role. The stray bullet that cut down General Joseph Johnston outside Richmond gave Lee a field command in June, 1862. Disaster was in the air. Kentucky had been lost. The Northern blockade was pinching, and King Cotton diplomacy was failing. By defeating General McClellan and relieving the pressure on Richmond, Lee opened up a new phase of American military history. The man who had spent his life at minor military posts would now show the world what kind of soldier he really was. No wonder a Pennsylvania girl said as Lee rode by, "I wish he were ours!" A tiger in battle, he never defended when he could attack. The victories that followed belong both to our history and folklore. Splendor and glory were his.

Yet as a field commander, he had a tragic flaw: the inability to shape opposing views to his purpose. Not once but three times did he yield to General Longstreet's obstinacy, agreeing to what he himself believed to be a second-best plan. Lee was too much of a gentleman to rank in battle beside a Caesar, a Napoleon, a Rommel, or—here we court heresy—a Grant. This was the lesson of Gettysburg, where Lee, with the greatest army ever under his command, was beaten by the smallest force Lincoln had fielded since 1861 when McDowell met Beauregard.

After the defeat, however, Lee did not look for a scapegoat. "It was all my fault," he said and wrote to Richmond, tendering his resignation. President Davis would not accept it. So Lee had to fight on to the inevitable end. Yet in the terrible winter of 1864, wonderful human touches shone through the days of despair. Attending church in Petersburg on February 5, Lee would not leave, despite word of a Yankee break-through, until after he had received Communion. Going up with the first group to the chancel, which was not his custom, he left as soon as possible and hurried to the battle line. New recruits were rushing about in disorder, and Lee tried to rally them.

"Great day, old man, get out of the way!" one terrified youth yelled. "You don't know nothing!" Lee went about his tasks without letting the lad know who he was.

Later on, a Negro appeared at the General's tent and was admitted. "General Lee," he began. "I been wantin' to see you for a long time. I's a soldier."

"Ah," said Lee, "with the Union or the Southern army?"

"I belongs to your army."

"Well, have you been shot?"

"No sah, I ain't been shot yet."

"How is that? Nearly all of our men get shot."

"Why, General, I ain't been shot 'case I stays back whar de generals stay." Lee not only enjoyed the reply then, he also repeated it to his staff on several occasions.

The long winter dragged on. The last Confederate port, Wilmington, North Carolina, was closed. President Davis became more authoritarian and autocratic. Openly criticized now by many of his own people, he lashed out at everyone, including Lee. Early in February, 1865, he telegraphed his commanding general who was struggling to hold Petersburg: "Rumor said to be based on orders given by you create concern and obstruct necessary legislation. Come over. I wish your views on the subject."

Thinking it would be catastrophic to leave Petersburg at that moment, Lee wired back in cipher: "Send me the measures and I will send you my views." The infuriated Davis dispatched a lengthy reply which ended: "Rest assured I will not ask your views in answer to measures. Your counsels are no longer wanted in this matter."

When Lee read this second telegram, he quietly ordered his horse, took the railroad train to Richmond and straightened out the matter. He was too big a man to match anger with anger. Shortly afterward he wrote to the President: "I know I am indebted to your indulgence and kind consideration for this honorable position. I must beg of you to continue these same feelings to me in the future and allow me to refer to you at all times for counsel and advice. I cannot otherwise hope to be of service to you or the country."

There is no better example of Lee sticking to the rules, and under the greatest possible stress and discouragement.

As the Southern cause waned that winter, Lee's reputation climbed. This is the most significant fact about Robert E. Lee's military career. Southern hopes focused on one man and the army he led. He was the embodiment of the cause that Southerners believed Providence would favor.

How could General Lee fail? The God who ruled all men would certainly bless him.

Precisely at this point, Lee assumed his unique role in American history. "As long as he could keep the field," wrote Douglas S. Freeman, "the South could keep its heart. So, when the despairing were ready to make peace, the loyal Confederate took his last horse from the stable and emptied his barn of corn in order that 'Lee's Army' might not starve."

When defeat finally came, Southerners believed it was their own bungling bureaucracy—not the Yankees—that had caused it. In his heart of hearts, Lee thought so, too. Of the Confederate Congress in Richmond, he once said: "They don't seem to be able to do anything except eat peanuts and chew tobacco while my army is starving." And again: "The only unfailing friend the Confederacy ever had was cornfield peas."

Confederate soldiers had one other unfailing friend—the head of the Army of Northern Virginia. His men were Lee's first obligation and his last hope. The power of his personality bound them together when everything else failed. What he believed, they would believe: what he ordered, they would do. Just before the final collapse at Appomattox, a faithful officer summed up the situation magnificently when Lee asked what the country would think if he abandoned the struggle.

"Country be damned," John S. Wise snapped back. "There is no country. There has been no country, General, for a year or more. You are the country to these men. They have fought for you. They have shivered through a long winter for you. Without pay or clothes, or care of any sort, their devotion to you and faith in you have been the only things which have held this army together. If you demand the sacrifice, there are still left thousands of us who will die for you."

After the surrender, this loyalty remained. On a long lonely ride north of Lexington, Lee met an old soldier who recognized him on Traveller.

"I feel like cheering you, General!"

"We're alone out here and the fighting is over. There's no reason to cheer me," Lee said.

"Guess ah'll jest cheer anyway." And so he did, loud and long, as Lee rode out of sight.

Lee had several other mounts during the Civil War—Richmond, Brown Roan, Ajax, Lucy Long; but the horse that won his heart and the imagination of posterity was Traveller. This animal became the Bucephalus of American history.

Traveller was no ordinary horse, any more than Lee was an ordinary general. The animal's strength, intelligence and bearing were notable. "Traveller walks as if he knew he bore a king on his back," an observer noted. Of Grey Eagle stock, Traveller was born in Greenbrier County, Virginia, in 1857. He was not a thoroughbred. "My horse was greatly admired by the soldiers for his springy walk, high spirit, and muscular strength," his original owner, Thomas L. Broun, wrote in 1861. "He never needs spur or whip, and will go anywhere."

Lee bought the colt for two hundred dollars, and kept Traveller for the rest of his life. The gray charger became as well known to the soldiers as his master. He was the most admired horse in a war which say the cavalry enjoy its final fling. Traveller survived all the battles and was with Lee at Gettysburg. He carried Lee home to Richmond, and to his new home in Lexington. Lee always took the horse to the blacksmith's shop himself, never trusting the job to a servant. Standing by Traveller's side, he would explain, "The bursting of bombs around him during the war made him nervous."

His own descriptions of Traveller were as lyrical as anything he ever wrote. "If I were an artist, I would draw his picture," he recorded, "representing his fine proportions, muscular figure, deep chest, short back, strong haunches, flat legs, small head, broad forehead, delicate ears, quick eye, small feet, and black mane and tail. Such a picture could inspire a poet, whose genius could then depict his worth and his endurance of toil, hunger, thirst, heat and cold, and the dangers and sufferings through which he passed. He might even imagine his thoughts through the long night-marches and the days of battle . . ." In his last years, Lee told how he and Traveller "wander in the mountains and enjoy sweet confidences." In a special way, this was the most revealing friendship of his whole life.

If Lee had a penchant for old horses, he had an even stronger one for young ladies. He delighted in kissing the girls, a prerogative he assumed with age. Here, too, Lee showed an affinity with certain of his Tidewater relatives. A cousin, Thomas H. Carter, habitually met incoming coaches, ardently kissed each young woman who stepped down and inquired gently: "What might your name be, dear: I think you're a kinswoman of mine."

To Lee's old-world courtesy and chivalry was added a slightly naughty but always harmless banter. Throughout his life he loved to assume the role of matchmaker. "Tell Miss _____ she had better dismiss the young divine and marry a soldier," he counseled a friend from Mexico.

"There is some chance of the latter being shot, but it requires a particular dispensation of Providence to rid her of the former."

This was the tone with which he approached his son's courtships, though underneath the surface Lee was very serious about matrimony. His October 26, 1867 letter to Robert, Jr. is a case in point. "I am clear for your marrying if you select a good wife," he wrote. "Otherwise you had better remain as you are for a time. An imprudent or uncongenial woman is worse than the minks." (The son had written that minks had destroyed his hens in a recent raid.)

Lee was obsessed with the all but endless ramifications of the Lee family: visits, courtships, births, betrothals, weddings, anniversaries, deaths. Quite naturally, this kept him in contact with many ladies. He knew his cousins to the third and fourth generation. To call him an Episcopal Shintoist is not unreasonable.

Females did not have to be Lees to catch his eye, however. "He has a good memory for pretty girls," a young man on his staff reported. "While in Savannah, one of my sisters sang for him. Afterward, in Virginia, almost as soon as he saw me he asked after his 'little singing bird.'"

Lee's letters to his daughters-in-law were always tender and usually fulsome. They bring home the point that Robert E. Lee was often a lonely man, isolated from his family by space and his associates by responsibility. Usually he contained himself on this score, but the passages alluding to this omnipresent loneliness are among the most touching in his letters. One such period came when he assumed his new position in Lexington. He had left his family east of the mountains, to follow him when conditions warranted the move. To them he wrote on October 9, 1865: "Life is indeed gliding away and I have nothing of good to show for mine that is past. I pray I may be spared to accomplish something for the benefit of mankind and the honor of God."

Among Lee's feminine correspondents, "Markie" ranks second only to Mrs. Lee. She was Martha Custis Williams, a great-niece of Mrs. Lee's father. "Markie," who had lived for many years at Arlington with her uncle, enjoyed Lee's warmest affection. Other persons in whom he confided were "Brit"—Mrs. Britannia Kennon, Mrs. Lee's first cousin; Mrs. Chapman Leigh and Miss Bell Harrison, two ladies who lived at Brandon; Maragaret and Caroline Stuart, both cousins; and Miss Norvell Caskie, a Richmond favorite of Lee, daughter of a wealthy tobacconist. Throughout the War, the General managed to answer in his own hand every letter sending him a present, and most personal letters as well. The glumness of the military situation was often concealed by the light-heartedness of his reply. "Last night when I reached my head-quarters, I found a card on my table with a hyacinth pinned to it," the General confided to Mrs. Roger A. Pryor. "The card read, 'For General Lee, with a kiss.' I have my hyacinth and my card—*and I mean to find my kiss!*"

Frequently he counseled young men about matters of the heart. His theme was consistent and persistent: faint heart never won fair lady. The advantage is with the offensive. When he himself lost the military offensive, he maintained that sweet, spontaneous courtesy which was his greatest weapon. As his beaten army staggered toward Appomattox, one woman, the wife of Dr. Guild, still accompanied the officers. The whole army was collapsing around him, but General Lee insisted on coming early every morning with a cup of coffee for Mrs. Guild, though he himself had none.

If Lee admired ladies, he loved children, and they him. When I myself came to Lexington in 1949, I met several octogenarians who had enjoyed a ride on Traveller at the General's request, and one who remembered making a daisy chain for the horse's neck. And once, a small girl, in charge of a recalcitrant young sister, saw Lee ride by and shouted, "Mr. Lee, I can't make Sister go home to Mother." The General rode Traveller over to the field of battle, picked up the little rebel Fannie, sat her beside him on the saddle and took her to her front door.

Far from Lexington, in the valleys and coves around about, children were awed and charmed by this "Apollo on Horseback." On a trip to the Peaks of Otter where he was climbing a steep rocky ascent, Lee met some little urchins with dirty faces playing near the road. He spoke to them pleasantly and said that a little water would improve their faces.

"They stared at us with open-eyed astonishment," wrote his daughter Mildred who was with her father. "Then they scampered off up the hill. A few minutes later, in rounding this hill, we passed a little cabin, when out they all ran with clean faces and their hair nicely brushed. One little girl exclaimed, 'We know you are General Lee. We've seen your picture!'"

Robert E. Lee was recognized and recognizable anywhere. Because he could treat everyone civilly, everyone trusted and admired him. His code was all of a piece, and it produced one complete person—a Christian gentleman. The two concepts are in part contradictory. The gentleman is bent on defending his life; the Christian gives his up to find a greater one. At the center of the gentleman is honor; of the Christian, humility. The pride which makes honor meaningful is, to Christian eyes, sinful. Some of this contradiction manifests itself in Lee's personality. How could he be such a furious warrior, and yet so gentle? How could he be so proud, and yet so humble? How could he accept all that happened so gracefully, and yet, in a sense, never accept it at all?

Lee's appeal, like his strength, exists on multiple levels. To those who only catch a glance of him riding across the pages of American history, he is the general on the beautiful horse, fighting bravely as did the knights of old. To Southerners, he is the chief patriot, defending his homeland with the last ounce of his strength. To the historian, he is a pivotal figure of the nineteenth century, a symbol of the revolt that almost wrecked the Ship of State. To the philosopher, he is the last major spokesman of the agrarian way of life which made the eighteenth century physiocrats the founding fathers of the nation. To the sociologist, he is the flower of a semi-feudalistic society built on caste and class.

To the poet, he is the silent enigma, the peerless Cavalier who made poetry out of action. To the educator, he is an early advocate of pragmatism and technical training in American universities. To the churchman, he is the fully committed Christian who put trust in God above all earthly things. To the genealogist, he is the epitome of one of the greatest American families, and the best proof that blood will tell. To the soldier, he is the man without a demerit who said that duty is the sublimest word in the English language. To the tourist, he is the man whose name seems to be on every road, every battlefield, and every victory south of the Potomac: the focal point for the cultural phenomenon known as the Civil War Centennial.

E pluribus unum: out of many, one. As with the nation he almost destroyed, so with the man. Out of all these traits the one figure emerges—a passionate man, filled with an unselfish passion that purifies rather than destroys. Though he fought for a section, he was not sectionalized by the conflict. He broke certain external rules so that he could adhere to internal rules which guided and governed him. He knew how to win and, more important, he knew how to lose. One might go further, and say that like most major figures, he was born to lose. For this reason his career—and his code—can be summarized in a single sentence. He undertook an impossible task, did the best he could, and was content to leave the rest to God.

This was the spirit in which Lee approached Lexington, and the way in which he conquered it. To change from a military to a civilian life when he was approaching sixty was difficult. He did it without whining or despairing. By Christmas, 1865, his routine had been firmly established. The College was functioning and growing. Despite all the problems on hand and those which were sure to come, no one doubted that Washington College would survive. Some were already insisting that it was destined to become a leading institution of higher learning. The Lee family was together now under one roof, surrounded by people who loved and respected them. The holiday festivities would not be lavish and memorable in the old Arlington–Stratford ante-bellum tradition. Compared to the Christmas of 1864, however, this one would be Elysian. Bright and gay, Robert E. Lee would reign like a patriarch. The one Christmas present he wanted more than anything else in the world had already been given him—the opportunity to fight for a difficult and honorable cause. Some order had been established in his shattered, disoriented world. He never had, and never would, ask for more than that.

VIII

THE HEARING

> It is not every question that
> deserves an answer.
> —Pubilius Syrus

THE YEAR 1866 opened with Lee sharpening his pencils in Lexington and Thaddeus Stevens sharpening his speeches in Washington. Before the winter was over, the Lee of reconciliation ran head on into the Stevens of vengeance in the Capitol Building. In its own way, the meeting was as dramatic as that of Lee and any of the Yankee generals who opposed him during the war itself.

January carried no indication of the approaching encounter so far as Lexington was concerned. A far more amenable Yankee than Stevens, Thomas Chapman of New York, took a large advertisement in the January 3 *Gazette*, offering to furnish free his vegetable balm recipe for removing "pimples, blotches, tan, freckles, etc." In the same issue, a local merchant demonstrated that the days of austerity were passing. He could now offer for sale French confectioneries: "Conversation Lozenges, Apple Jelly Bonbons, and Citron." If a cloud of numbness and nostalgia still hung over the valley, there were rays of sunlight coming through as well. The January 10 *Gazette* carried the joyful news that Cyrus McCormick, a local lad who had reaped huge profits in Chicago, planned to give ten thousand dollars to Washington College, making possible a new chair in Experimental Philosophy and Practical Mechanics. Agents of the College, soliciting money from the South's conquerors, reported considerable success. The New York *Daily News* was quoted as saying: "We greatly mistake the feeling of New York if its wealthy men of business and retired men of fortune will not embrace this occasion to support General Lee's school."

Further north, in Boston, a different outlook on the affairs of the day could be detected. "Now is the critical time," wrote Wendell Phillips. "The rebellion has not ceased, it has only changed its weapons. Once it fought; now it intrigues. Once it followed Lee in arms; now it follows Johnson in guile and chicanery." And the Boston *Transcript* was so angered by Andrew Johnson's speeches that it even advocated the abolition of the Presidential office.

In order to check and, if necessary, destroy President Johnson's program, Congress set up a Joint Committee on Reconstruction. Thaddeus Stevens was chairman. Of the fifteen members, twelve were ardent Republicans. Among them were some of the most bitter and implacable foes of the South. This group largely determined the course of future federal policies on reconstruction.

By reading the testimony of the one hundred forty-four witnesses called before the committee, anyone can discover that the investigators had reached a number of firm conclusions before they opened their hearings. Over half the witnesses were Northerners living in the South; many of them had been in trouble or disrepute there. Others gave spectacular accounts of Southern cruelty: of shooting Negroes in cold blood, tying women up by the thumbs, and "bucking and gagging" any who dared talk back. In short, to demonstrate that the program advocated by Johnson would lead to "madness and folly" was the committee's main task. If, at the same time, it could harass former Rebel leaders, so much the better. No wonder the Lexington *Gazette* reported with little enthusiasm in the February 14, 1866 issue: "General Lee has been summoned to appear before the Congressional Reconstruction Committee and, we believe, he starts for Washington this morning."

If the white-haired warrior thought his strenuous battles were over, he was mistaken. Now he must rally his words, not his artillery, to stand off the enemy.

"Are you acquainted with the state of feeling among Virginia's secessionists toward the government of the United States?"

"I have been living very retired, and have had but little communication with politicians."

February 17, 1866. The Capitol, Washington, D.C. General Lee sat for two hours in the Committee Room of the Joint Committee on Reconstruction, to answer questions and explain his former actions.

He had faced few meetings in his whole life with such distaste. Lee saw no reason to open old wounds. He anticipated no gains from such a meeting and sensed great potential losses. He could not keep a look of lofty disdain, tinged with a suggestion of disquietude, from stealing over his face.

Though he did indeed have "little communication with politicians," Lee knew a good deal about the chairman of the committee, Thaddeus Stevens. A bitter old man of seventy-six now, fifteen years Lee's senior, Stevens circled over Southern history like a hungry hawk. His radical and bitter policies, combined with his vindictive temper and flare for invective, had made him a unique and sinister character.

Acknowledged leader of the House, on December 4, 1865, he had made the motion that set up the Reconstruction Committee. His view was unequivocal: the South was a conquered province with which Congress could do as it pleased. Stevens made no effort to hide the fact that one of his aims was "to continue the Republican ascendency." Whenever his followers hesitated, he rallied them with invective, insinuations, threats, taunts and cracks of the party whip. He would chastise party and President alike if either dared to stand in his way.

Fortunately for Lee, Stevens himself did not conduct the February 17 hearing. That task was left to the sixty-one-year-old senator from Michigan, Jacob M. Howard. Born in Shaftsbury, Vermont, educated at Bennington and Brattleboro, Howard stood with Stevens in favoring extreme punishment for the South. Becoming a leader of the Michigan bar while still a young man, Howard had been first a Whig, then a Republican. An eloquent speaker, ponderous and pontifical, he won fame before the Civil War as attorney general of Michigan. Since 1862 he had stood with the radicals in the United States Senate. During the war years Howard was on the judiciary and military affairs committees. As a member of the former, he drafted the first clause of the Thirteenth Amendment. Assigned the job of investigating Reconstruction in Virginia and the Carolinas, he sought national acclaim by waving the bloody shirt and confounding the ex-rebels. The single word on which he centered his program—other senators in the twentieth century would one day imitate him in this—was *loyalty*. If he could only make Lee lose his temper and shout defiance at the conquerors, the victory would be Howard's.

"From your observation," the senator continued, "what is the feeling of secessionists toward our government?"

Today Lee, the fighter, did not intend to attack. Showing marked restraint, he avoided the blows by stepping aside. "So far as has come to my knowledge, I do not know of a single person who either feels or contemplates any resistance."

"Is it then your opinion that they are *friendly* towards the government of the United States?" Howard was determined to push Lee beyond his neutral position. Obviously most rebels were not friendly toward their recent enemies. Had he claimed this, Lee would have appeared obsequious.

"I believe they entirely *acquiesce* in the government," he replied. "So far as I have heard any one express an opinion, they are for co-operating with President Johnson in his policy." Lee had suddenly taken the offensive; most of the committee members were enraged by Johnson's reconciliatory moves.

"In his policy in regard to what?"

"His policy in regard to the restoration of the whole country. People have expressed great confidence in the wisdom of his policy of restoration."

"How do they feel in regard to that portion of the people of the United States who have been forward and

THE HEARING

zealous in the prosecution of the war against the rebellion?"

"Well, I do not know. I have heard nobody express any opinion in regard to it. As I said before, I have not had much communication with politicians in the country, if there are any."

"How do the secessionists feel in regard to the payment of the United States debt contracted in the prosecution of the war?"

"I have never heard any one speak on the subject. I suppose they must expect to pay the taxes levied by the government."

"If the question were left to them, would they repudiate and reject that debt?"

Both Howard and Lee knew they would. What people have ever been anxious to pay for the very instruments that destroyed them? Lee avoided an evasive answer without resorting to falsehood or equivocation. He spoke of Southern character rather than opinion.

"I never heard anyone speak on that subject, but from my knowledge of the people I believe that they would be in favor of the payment of all *just* debts."

Now it was up to the Senator to define "just debts." Instead of answering, he threw the question back at Lee.

"Do they, in your opinion, regard that as a just debt?"

"I do not know what their opinion is on the subject of the particular debt. I believe that the people would pay the debts they are called upon to pay. I say that from my knowledge of the people generally."

"Would they pay that debt with as much alacrity as people ordinarily pay their taxes to their government?"

"I do not know that they would make any distinction between the two. The taxes laid by the government, so far as

I know, they are prepared to pay to the best of their ability. I never heard them make any distinction."

"What about paying the so-called Confederate debt?"

"I believe, so far as my opinion goes, they would be willing to pay the Confederate debt too."

"You think they would?"

We would like to know the manner in which the Senator asked this—quizzically, sarcastically, incredulously? Whatever the implication, Lee answered in the straightforward manner which was his best weapon.

"I think they would if they had the power and ability to do it. I have never heard any one in the state with whom I have conversed speak of repudiating any debt."

"I suppose the Confederate debt is almost entirely valueless?"

"Entirely, as far as I know."

"Do you recollect the terms of the Confederate bonds—when they were made payable?"

"I think I have a general recollection that they were made payable six months after a declaration of peace."

"Six months after the ratification of a treaty of peace between the United States and the Confederate government?"

"I think they ran in that way."

"So that the bonds are not due yet by their terms?"

"I suppose, unless it is considered that there is peace now, they are not due."

Here Lee revealed himself not only a cautious witness but an astute legalist. He refused to be forced either into repudiating or endorsing the Confederate debt, or even the terms of payment. Well over six months had passed since he signed the surrender papers in Appomattox, but he

The fading vision of classical splendor shone through the battered buildings to which Lee came in 1865. Washington College façade, 1868.

Powhatan Co. 24 Aug '65

Gentlemen

I have delayed for some days, replying to your letter of the 5th Inst: informing me of my election by the Board of Trustees, to the Presidency of Washington College, from a desire to give the subject due consideration. Fully impressed with the responsibilities of the office, I have feared that I should be unable to discharge its duties, to the satisfaction of the Trustees, or to the benefit of the Country. The proper education of youth requires not only great ability, but I fear more strength than I now possess, for I do not feel able to undergo the labour of conducting classes in regular Courses of instruction. I could not therefore undertake more than the general administration & supervision of the Institution. There is another subject which has caused me serious reflection, & is I think worthy of the consideration of the Board. Being excluded from the terms of amnesty in the proclamation of the President of the U.S. of the 29 May last, & an object of censure to a portion of the Country, I have thought it probable that my occupation of the position of President, might draw upon the College a feeling of hostility; & I should therefore cause injury to an Institution, which it would be my highest desire to advance. I think it the duty of every citizen in the present condition of the Country, to do all in his power to aid in the restoration of peace, harmony, & in no way to oppose the policy of the State or Gen'l Governments, directed to that object. It is particularly incumbent on those charged with the instruction of the young, to set them an example of submission to authority, & I could not consent to be the cause of animadversion upon the College.

Should you however take a different view, & think that my services in the position tendered me by the Board will be advantageous to the College & Country, I will yield to your judgement & accept it. Otherwise I must most respectfully decline the office.

Begging you to express to the trustees of the College my heartfelt gratitude for the honor conferred upon me, & requesting you to accept my cordial thanks for the kind manner in which you have communicated its decision,

I am Gentlemen with great respect
your most Obt Sevt
R E Lee

Messrs John W. Brockenbrough Rector
S. McD. Reid, Alfred Leyburn
Horatio Thompson D.D. Bolivar Christian } Committee
J. J. Kirkpatrick

Lee's letter accepting the presidency of Washington College

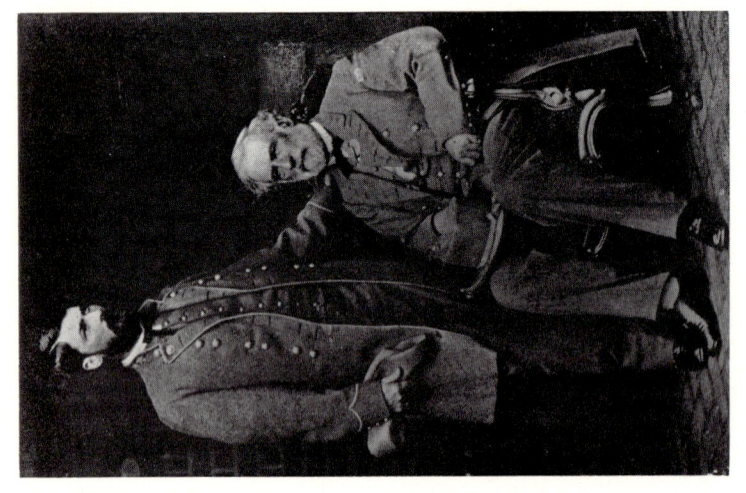

Brady's famous 1865 Richmond picture of Lee and his son Custis

General Francis Smith, one of Lee's closest Lexington friends

Lee mounted on Traveller was one of the most popular pictures in the post-war South. It was made in Lee's Lexington backyard.

Esthetically speaking, the Lees were thoroughly Victorian. Here is their Lexington living room.

The General's beloved wife was a chronic invalid, and an unreconstructed rebel.

General Lee's office, just as it looked the last time he saw it

Lee built this home for himself and his family on the Washington College campus.

Lee passed this tranquil spot many times on his long country rides.

Lexington's Main Street during Lee's last years

Lee's funeral procession wends its way down Lexington's Main Street.

Washington College campus on the day Lee was buried (reproduced from an old glass plate partially destroyed)

All around him General Lee saw faces from an Old South that lived only in memory.

Valentine's statue of the recumbent Lee now rests in Lee Chapel.

Both the anguish and the triumph of Lee's closing years emerged in this remarkable photograph by Michael Miley.

would not equate this with a treaty of peace. He insisted that the Senator define what he meant by "peace."

Instead of doing this, Lee's inquisitor moved to another critical area—race relationships in the chaotic South. Here he found Lee more willing to express firm opinions but not to draw moral implications.

"How do you feel in regard to the education of the blacks?"

"Where I am, and have been, the people have exhibited a willingness that the blacks should be educated, and they express an opinion that that would be better for the blacks and better for the whites."

"General, you are very competent to judge of the capacity of black men for acquiring knowledge. I want your opinion on that capacity, as compared with the capacity of white men."

"I am not particularly qualified to speak on that subject, as you seem to intimate; but I do not think that he is as capable of acquiring knowledge as the white man is. There are some more apt than others." What Lee feared most, it seemed, was "opening the door to a great deal of demagogism," an inherent danger in the Reconstruction South.

"General, are you aware of the existence among the blacks of Virginia of plans to disturb the peace?"

"I am not. I have seen no evidence of it, and have heard of none."

Senator Howard moved next to one of his favorite questions, in the area of foreign affairs: "In the event of a war between the United States and any foreign power, if the recently rebel states were given a fair prospect of gaining their independence and shaking off the government of the

United States, is it, or is it not, your opinion that they would avail themselves of the opportunity?"

"I have nothing whatever to base an opinion upon. So far as I know, they contemplate nothing of the kind now. What may happen in the future I cannot say."

"Do you not frequently hear in your intercourse with secessionists expressions of a hope that such a war may break out?"

"I cannot say that I have. On the contrary, I have heard persons express a hope that the country may *not* be led into a war."

"If war came, would the people whom I call secessionists join the common enemy?"

"It is possible. It depends upon the feelings of the individual."

"What, in such an event, might be your own choice?"

One can just imagine how quiet and tense the room must have become when this question was asked.

"I have no disposition now to do it, and I never have had."

"And can you foresee that such would be your inclination in such an event?"

"No. I can only judge by the past. I cannot pretend to foresee events."

If the Senator could not find fault with Lee's attitudes about the future, he could at least bring up a public act of the past: "Did you not take an oath of fidelity to the Confederate government?"

"I do not recollect having done so; but it is possible that, when I was commissioned, I did. I do not recollect whether it was required, or, if it was required, I took it. If it had been required, I would have taken it; but I do not recollect whether it was or not."

Not since the hearings had begun had a witness handled himself with such consummate skill. Undoubtedly Senator Howard was impressed and perhaps exasperated, too. Up to Lee's appearance, matters had gone extremely well for him. John B. Baldwin, speaker of the Virginia House of Delegates and a "thorough-going Union man," had given all the "right" answers. So had William J. Dews, "uniformly a Union man," who roundly denounced President Johnson's plans, and complained that in Staunton, just thirty-four miles from Lee's new home, "the citizens regard a Union man about as they do a nigger." Mr. Dews revealed that he was so angered by local attitudes that he had written to the Union commander in Charlottesville asking him whether, "if it became necessary, he would be prepared to start some troops up to Staunton by train"—an act that could hardly have enhanced Dew's local position with ex-Confederates.

On February 15, Howard had questioned John Minor Botts, one of Virginia's leading Unionist politicians. After a full account of his own laudable acts, Botts warned the Committee that Lee's name had been suggested for governor. The suggestion had been greeted in Richmond "with great applause, both in the galleries and on the floor." Botts concluded with a strong denunciation of President Johnson: "The sooner he retraces his steps, as far as it is possible, the better it will be for him, the South, and the nation."

That same afternoon, Colonel Orland Brown, Assistant Commissioner in Richmond's Bureau of Freedmen, Refugees, and Abandoned Lands, had given another strongly pro-Union interpretation of the Virginia scene. During his testimony, Howard asked how Southerners regarded General Lee. "With the highest affection," Brown answered. "I know of no man who has more fully the hearts of a people than he."

Now General Lee himself faced Howard, but the Senator could not seem to hold his own, let alone squelch him. So in order to regroup for a later charge, he allowed his colleagues to take over the hearing.

One of these was thirty-seven-year-old Roscoe Conkling, who built up his body by systematic exercise and boxing so he could continue to be called "the finest torso in public life." Beefy and ambitious, he was already a noted "spread-eagle" orator. Married to the sister of New York's Governor Horatio Seymour and mayor of Utica before entering Congress, Conkling was a figure to be reckoned with. In the tense months before secession, when Massachusett's Senator Sumner was caned in the Senate, Conkling stood beside the crippled Thaddeus Stevens to serve as his defender. In 1867 he still supported the Stevens who would harry the rebels out of the land. And now across the table sat the noblest rebel of them all.

Another questioner was forty-nine-year-old Henry T. Blow. Throughout the hearings he tended to live up to his name. Unlike Howard and Conkling, Blow was of Southern extraction. Thirteen when his moderately successful planter father left Virginia for the midwest, Henry had attended school and college at St. Louis. A pioneer in the expanding lead-mining field, he had become wealthy and was welcomed into the ranks of the Whigs. Conservative and powerful, he helped to organize the Republican party in Missouri, and attended the 1860 national convention as a delegate. Rewarded for his support by being sent as minister to Venezuela, Blow returned in 1862 to run for Congress as a "Charcoal"—one who favored the immediate and uncompensated emancipation of Missouri's slaves. His support of Thaddeus Stevens' radical policies won him various political plums, including a place on the Reconstruction Committee. Having listened carefully to the Senator's questions, Blow now began his own by harping back to one of Lee's answers.

"If President Johnson's policies were adopted, would there be anything like the old feeling? I notice you spoke of 'acquiescing in the result.' "

"I believe it would take time for the feelings of the people to be of that cordial nature to the government that they were formerly."

"Do you think that their preference for that policy arises from a desire to have peace, or from the probability of their regaining political power?"

Here was a loaded question, but Lee was determined not to lose his temper or his advantage.

"So far as I know the desire of the people of the South, it is for the restoration of their civil government. They look upon the policy of President Johnson as the one which would most clearly and most surely re-establish it."

From a series of additional rounds about politics, economics and race relations, Lee emerged with dignity and calmness.

Senator Howard eventually broke in to press for an admission which Lee refused to make: "Is there not a general dislike of northern men among secessionists?"

"I suppose they would prefer not to associate with them," Lee admitted, adding wryly, "I do not know that they would select them as associates. I think it probable they would not admit them into their social circles."

Representative Blow then asked more questions about

Johnson's "soft" reconstruction policy. Lee continued to defend it without vehemence and to answer questions without antagonism.

After a short recess, Senator Howard took over again, asking if the "once rebel states had the opportunity to secede again, would they avail themselves of that opportunity?"

"I suppose it would depend upon the circumstances existing at the time," replied Lee. "If their feelings should remain embittered, and their affections alienated from the rest of the states, I think it very probable they might do so, provided they thought it was to their interest."

"Is there not a deep-seated feeling of disappointment in the South over the outcome of the war?"

"I think that, at the time, they were disappointed at the result of the war."

"Do you think it would be practicable to convict a man in Virginia of treason for having taken part in this rebellion against the government?"

Again Lee avoided a blunt and negative answer by pleading his own ignorance of current attitudes and by turning the question back on the questioner: "On that point I have no knowledge, and I do not know what they would consider treason against the United States."

At this point, Senator Howard became annoyed. He tried to intensify the question by narrowing it. "You understand my question. Suppose a jury was impaneled in your own neighborhood. Would it be practicable to convict Jefferson Davis for having levied war against the United States, and thus having committed the crime of treason?"

"I think it very probable that they would not consider he had committed treason."

Not satisfied with this admission, the Senator pushed the point further: "Suppose the jury should be clearly and plainly instructed by the court that such an act on the part of Mr. Davis constituted in itself the crime of treason—would the jury be likely to heed that instruction?"

"I do not know, sir, what they would do on that question."

"They do not generally suppose that it was treason against the United States, do they?"

"I do not think that they would so consider it." Pressed further, Lee then said that he thought most Southerners believed secession had been the responsibility of the states rather than of individuals.

After this, the Senator asked: "What are your own personal views on this question?"

"That was my view: that the act of Virginia, in withdrawing herself from the United States, carried me along as a citizen of Virginia; her laws and her acts were binding on me."

"*That* you felt to be your justification in taking the course you did?"

"Yes, sir."

"I have been told, General, that you have remarked to some of your friends in conversation that you were rather wheedled or cheated into that course by politicians?"

Plainly Senator Howard was prodding. Words like "wheedled" and "cheated" did not pass often from the lips of Lee.

"I do not recollect making any such remark. I do not think I ever made it."

The conversation continued in a political vein. Lee was asked how his people would respond to a Constitutional amendment enfranchising all the former slaves. His answer was a masterpiece of understatement.

"I think, so far as I can form an opinion, in such an opinion they would object."

"If it were adopted, nevertheless, would it lead to scenes of violence and breaches of the peace?"

"I think it would excite unfriendly feelings between the two races. I cannot pretend to say to what extent it would go, but that would be the result."

"Are you acquainted with the proposed amendment now pending in the Senate of the United States?"

"No sir, I am not. I scarcely ever read a paper."

The Honorable Mr. Blow took over again now, after an explanation by Roscoe Conkling of the proposed Thirteenth Amendment. Lee sat quietly, making no comment. He answered a series of questions on racial manners cautiously but firmly, refusing to admit that the situation was "out of hand" in Virginia. He would not play the role of demagogue. Senator Howard resumed his questions, bringing up one of the day's most inflammable issues—the mistreatment of Northern prisoners in Southern prisons.

"While you were in command at Richmond, did you know of the cruelties practiced toward the Union prisoners at Libby Prison and Belle Isle?"

"I never knew that any cruelty was practiced, and I have no reason to believe that it was practiced. I can believe, and have reasons to believe, that privations may have been experienced among the prisoners. I know that provisions and shelter could not be provided them."

"Were you not aware that men were dying from cold and starvation?"

Aware? *Aware? Was* I aware? The questions must have

bitten like strong acid. In those vivid and unspoken images that crowded through Lee's mind that moment and on other days, what did he see, what did he feel? What reveries of the past found their way into that crowded committee room less than a year after Lee's men manned their lines before Petersburg?

The historian cannot rightly draw upon reverie; but to think that the real marrow of the hearing got into the stenographer's notes is to be more naive than one might want to be.

At this point Senator Howard took it upon himself to deliver a little speech. He wanted the record of the hearings to show that "it was useless to conceal the fact that those prison scenes have created a sad feeling in the hearts of all Northern people." He wanted all the people back in Michigan to know that he was pushing their grievances with a Jehovah-like vengeance.

When the opportunity arose, Lee said quietly, "I had no control over the prisoners, once they had been sent to Richmond. I never gave an order about it. This was entirely in the hands of the War Department."

"And not in your hands?"

"Not in mine."

"Did not these scenes come at all to your knowledge?"

"Never. No report was ever made to me about them. There was no call for any to be made to me. Prisoners suffered from the want of ability on the part of the Confederate states to supply their wants. As far as I could, I did everything in my power to relieve them, and urged the formation of a cartel."

Pushed further, Lee told of specific proposals made to Grant, and of the work of his Christian Committee. He would not admit for a moment that his policy had been cruel or vindictive. Though he could bend like a willow on political questions outside his province, Lee stood like an oak on matters of military policy and conduct. "Orders were that the whole field should be treated alike," he said. "We took in the Federal wounded as well as ours on every field."

His inquisitors were getting nowhere. They decided to change the subject.

"I suppose most Negroes at this time are able to work. But there are helpless ones among them?" asked Mr. Blow.

"Certainly. I do not know to what extent." Lee had been for gradual emancipation. He refused to defend chattel slavery.

"Is there any other matter which you desire to state now?" Senator Howard asked.

"No, sir," Lee replied, "though I am ready to answer any questions which you think proper to me."

Thus the hearing ended.

Weeks later the *Joint Report* of the Committee would lash out at the South, showing none of Lee's calm magnanimity and fairness. "The Rebels heaped every imaginable insult and injury upon our nation," it would proclaim. "They fought for four years with the most determined and malignant spirit . . . and are today unrepentant and unpardoned."

An hysterical note would mar the conclusion of what was supposedly an impartial and empirical hearing: "The anti-coercive policy which allowed the rebellion to take form and gather force would be surpassed in infamy by the matchless wickedness that would now surrender the halls of Congress to those so recently in rebellion . . ."

The emotional excesses of the report would be matched by those of the Southerners when they read it. In Lee's new residence, Lexington, the editor of the *Gazette* lashed out with unusual vehemence. The "devilish iniquity and malignant wickedness" of the Committee's report he found "so monstrous that no Southern man can read it without invoking the righteous indignation of heaven." How long was the South to suffer from such wretched injustice and perfidy? Still in its first year of rebirth after invasion and collapse, the *Gazette* concluded with words of finality and defiance: "Under no conceivable circumstances will we concur in the adoption of the Constitutional amendment proposed by the Reconstruction Committee. *This is a fixed fact.*"

Thus, Lee, the reconciler, was caught between two adamant positions: that of his former enemies and that of his former Confederates. The razor-sharp rancor of both camps cut deep into his soul. In his private letters, he occasionally let a little of his despair show through. Writing home about his trip to Washington, he admitted: "I am now considered such a monster that I hesitate to darken with my shadow the doors of those I love best, lest I should bring them misfortune."

Back in Lexington, Lee watched and worked while Stevens and his cohorts overwhelmed Andrew Johnson and his program. On April 9, 1866, the Civil Rights Bill passed over the President's veto.

"What will happen to us now?" Mrs. Lee wrote to a friend. No one had the answer.

As debts accumulated, stay laws were passed throughout Dixie to ward off catastrophe. Mississippi suspended for two years its laws covering collection of debts. Georgia suspended indefinitely the sale of property for debt. South Carolina abolished imprisonment for debt and prevented foreclosure.

But if conditions were bad for the white man, they were much worse for the destitute Negroes. Many people actually thought that, under the circumstances, they would not be able to survive. The editor of the Natchez *Democrat* wrote: "The child is already born who will behold the last Negro in the state of Mississippi."

Signs of rebellion began to crop up again. Confederate flags were peddled openly in a dozen cities and were called "sacred souvenirs" by Alabama's Governor Parsons. "Stonewall Jackson soup" and "Confederate hash" appeared on hotel menus. In Richmond, a magazine called *The Land We Love* began to glorify the "Lost Cause."

Open conflicts between racial groups spread. Three days of rioting in Memphis, beginning on April 30, left forty-six Negroes dead and scores of homes, churches and schools burned. Summer riots in New Orleans saw sensational and unsavory actions go unchecked. Visiting reporters told of the stabbing and head-smashing tactics used on many already wounded or killed by policemen. Murder degenerated into massacre. "The hands of the rebel are again red with loyal blood," proclaimed the New York *Tribune*.

Everywhere President Johnson, determined to take his case directly to the people, was greeted with scorn and rudeness. In Pittsburgh and Indianapolis, he was literally driven off the platform. In Chicago he was greeted by a sign reading: NO WELCOME TO TRAITORS.

Lee and most Southerners realized that politically conditions had become much worse, not better, since Appomattox. Instead of stepping into the arena, Lee worked quietly and persistently at his own job as president of his small, independent college. For him and his region, the battle would be longer and harder than he had hoped. But Lee was used to long hard battles. He would confront the paper work and the problems as they came in. In the final hearing, that would be his best, and his only, defense.

IX

THE OFFICE

> Infinite riches in a little room.
> —Christopher Marlowe

OFFICES ARE silent biographers of those who spend much of their lives in them. Books, papers, pictures, furniture, little crumbled nothings, stuffed in drawers give the measure of the man. Beginning as inanimate rooms, offices become organic spaces, with personalities and meaning of their own. Things thought, filed, and remembered in them somehow capture the whole drama of life—the hopes, heartaches, failures and triumphs.

Robert E. Lee is gone, but his office is intact. After his death, college officials decided to preserve it exactly as it was when he walked out for the last time on a soggy fall day in 1870. No major item has been added or removed. Time has been blacked out and history boxed in.

Before setting up an office, Lee insisted on building a chapel for Washington College. On July 18, 1866, the trustees authorized the construction of a chapel, "not to exceed in cost $10,000." The plan and actual building received the President's closest attention. A quaint Victorian structure with a flared central tower, it added Gothic trimmings to Romanesque windows, showing little aesthetic distinction. There were five double sash windows on each side, with two more in front. Pine floors and bricks kilned nearby gave a local flavor to the building that was destined to become the shrine for the man who sponsored it. The dedication ceremonies for the new chapel took place during the June commencement exercises in 1867.

Lee's office is in the basement of that chapel. To get to it, one takes the narrow cast-iron stairs descending from the front of the church. Three sharp turns give the twenty-four steps the appearance of a corkscrew. Daylight streams through the diamond-shaped panes of Victorian glass in the single large stairwell window. One naked electric light bulb shines at night, placed where an oil lamp hung in Lee's day. The brick floor at the foot of the stairs has been cracked and worn by the feet of many pilgrims. Two steps down from this space is a larger brick floor, underneath a brick barrel vault. Twenty feet further on is a door leading onto the college campus. Off to the right, under another brick archway, is General Lee's office.

To the modern eye, the fifteen by eighteen foot room seems plain to the point of austerity. There is no rug on the pine floor of random-width boards, no curtains on the two windows, no paintings or prints on the plain white walls. To the small fireplace in the far corner, a squat cast-iron stove is attached by a tin stovepipe. The main exposed ceiling beam has been covered and painted white.

The furnishings reflect the era and the man. The unmatched Victorian pieces would be of little value to an antique dealer or connoisseur. The largest object in the room is a book case, originally a sideboard. Given by an admiring Virginia lady, Miss Upshur, the heavy case is adorned with Doric columns, a wall of troy fringe and four gilded lion's feet. Only one of the glass-enclosed shelves contains books: it is not full. Webster's *Dictionary* is the largest volume. Most of the others were nineteenth-century texts: De Vere's *Grammar in French*, Brown's *English Grammar with Analysis*, Morris' *Greek Grammar* and Downes' *Algebra*, for example. All are frayed and worn from frequent use.

In the center of the room is a veneered table with a glass top. Under the glass, pens, ink, string and various neatly arranged office items may be seen. The walnut secretary, also of ornate Victorian design, stands against the far wall. Lee's palm fan still rests on it. The chairs in the room are plain with wicker bottoms, except for Lee's own chair which is leather. This and the leather couch under the window were gifts of ladies at Miss Brown's Seminary in Lynchburg. Under one of the windows is an end-table. On it rests a double-pronged oil lamp.

One single object hangs from the walls: a map of Augusta County, drawn for the Board of Survey of Washington College by "Jed." Hotchkiss and signed "R. E. Lee, Pres. of Bd. of Survey." On the mantel stand three faded pictures: George Peabody a Northern benefactor, an unidentified Confederate family, and George Washington. Underneath the central table is a large wicker waste basket, given to General Lee by a Negro woman. This is all one finds in the office of the American who is regarded by many as a sort of Protestant saint.

Across the hall, a few feet from the office, the earthly remains of Lee are sealed in the family mausoleum. Above him rests his wife. To his right is his father, "Light Horse Harry"; to his left his oldest son, Custis. The General is entombed not far from the place where he worked and where he led in peace a whole region which he could not free in war.

This was the focus and nerve center of his administration. Here he wrote, planned, conferred, and meted out justice. He poured energy, devotion and judgment into this room and the people who visited it. "I have about a bushel of letters to answer and other things to do," he once wrote, but he never complained. Duty, like marrow, was in his bones. Precisely here the college was transformed into a university.

Like his clothes, speech, manners and campaigns, the office, too, was fastidious. A passion for order dominated Lee's whole life. "His specialty," one of the teachers of his youth recalled, "was finishing up." Lee finished up his life, as he had all his activities, with a tidiness that challenged belief.

Rising early, he held his private prayers, after which he went promptly to breakfast which was generally delayed by his tardy wife. There were family prayers at this morning meal as well. Lee ate heartily and left promptly for the seven forty-five chapel service. Lectures began at eight o'clock. By then, he would have slipped downstairs to his office. Sitting at the neat table, he started immediately to take care of his paper-kingdom tasks, many of which he must have found far from palatable.

President Lee depended on a system of meetings and reports that turned Washington College into a tightly organized school. Faculty members had to report every week on every student. Lee both tabulated and remembered the comments and grades. Soon after the grades were known, Lee arranged to see those who were doing poorly, sending Lewis, the college janitor, to their rooms with notes. At the end of the month, full records of standing were posted. Those who were to appear before him had their names marked. He also kept up with absences, and his signature was on all reports sent to parents. He attended many daily class recitations. "I recited in the presence of General Lee many times. It was a severe ordeal," C. A. Graves, an ex-student, remembered. "I have often wondered how he found the patience to endure the many hours of attendance on the many classes."

In addition to struggling with the students, Lee dealt day by day with the financial distress of the College. As we have already seen, he had to oversee the smallest items of repair, building or purchasing. Every penny counted. Lee knew this, and impressed it on everyone who came within his ken.

The Trustee's report of June 20, 1865, noted the considerable damage done by General Hunter's raid. Later conditions became worse, "owing to the want of material and means for making repairs, and partly to the impossibility of closing buildings against the depredations of mischievous persons." The following February the treasurer was authorized to have certain shelves installed, "provided the carpenter would agree to wait for money until the opening of the next session." Working capital simply was not to be had.

With these and other problems Lee wrestled throughout the morning. Any gifts or favors were promptly and painstakingly acknowledged. Constitutionally averse to adjectives, Lee could become fulsome when thanking a donor.

After Warren Newcomb of New York endowed ten scholarships, Lee wrote: "Those contributing to this great result will be ranked by posterity among the most meritorious citizens." Books donated by Rathmell Wilson would, he wrote, "do much for the advancement of science, give an impulse to the spread and development of that knowledge so highly valued by your esteemed brother, and cause his memory to be revered and cherished by the wise and good."

Working steadily and swiftly, Lee tried to finish his office work most days by early afternoon. He did not like to eat his second meal of the day until all his chores were finished. After lunch he usually slept, often napping upright in his chair. The afternoon belonged to Traveller, the town, and the countryside.

"He was very fond of horseback journeys," Robert Jr. wrote, "and enjoyed the quiet and rest, the freedom of mind and body, the close sympathy of his old war-horse, and the beauties of Nature which are to be seen at every turn in the mountains of Virginia."

These jaunts gave him "abundant opportunity for quiet thought." His favorite road led through the picturesque and rugged countryside between Lexington and Rockbridge Baths. If there were calls to be made to the newly arrived or to the sick, this was the time he made them.

Precisely at dusk he would be back home, ready for supper. The evening hours were for his family and guests. At ten he began to lock up the house. Young men courting his daughters had to respond accordingly. After that, the General was ready to go up to the bed over which hung his army pistol in its leather holster. Soon he fell into a quiet sleep. Another day would have ended.

The drama of these twilight years was internal. Hence it

has been harder to perceive and appreciate than that of the war years. The man who had moved armies was concerned now with moving papers. They became the central concern of his life. "I can go in the dark, and lay my hand on any particular paper in my office," he once said.

This is not to imply that President Lee was a scholar, a writer or reader: he was not. If he had any desire to begin any research of his own, he never said so. The idea of collecting material for wartime memoirs came to nothing. His own sentences reveal occasional errors in grammar and syntax. He was given to a flavorless military narrative style. What he wrote officially became ponderous and dull, and his one major effort—a thirty-four thousand word introduction to his father's memoirs—cannot be described as effective writing.

On several occasions Lee stated that he seldom read newspapers. His letters contain a single reference to the Washington *Star*, one to *The New York Times*, one to the *Watchman*, and a few casual references to other papers. That and no more. Lee told a Scotch visitor, David Macrae, that he had never read a history of the Civil War or the biography of anyone who fought in it. "My own life has been written, but I have not looked into it," Lee added. "I do not wish to awaken memories of the past."

If he did not arouse past history, he did not pursue current trends much, either. This is all the more notable considering his advice to his daughter Mildred: "Read history, works of truth, not novels and romances. Get correct views of life and learn to see the world in its true light."

The name of Shakespeare never occurs in Lee's letters. He had no bent toward drama or fiction. Since his private library was very meager after the war, he had to depend on those of Washington College and the Franklin Society. By checking the existing records, we are able to find out how few books Lee borrowed. We also have this quotation from Dr. E. C. Gordon, librarian of Washington College in the late 1860's: "General Lee never talked with me about books. I do not recall ever seeing him in the Library ... He was, of course, a member of the Franklin Society. I never saw him at any of the meetings." Apparently Lee checked out less than fifty books from the two libraries during his years in Lexington. Interestingly enough, a marked change occurred in his reading after 1867. From that time on, he borrowed no more books on American history or biography.

Not by reading but by doing, did Lee change the college he had come to guide. Before the war, there had been only four professors, teaching six subjects: mental and moral philosophy, political economy, Latin, Greek, mathematics and physical sciences. A decidedly religious tone prevailed. Although the school was non-denominational, morning and evening chapel were required of all students to encourage "the controlling influence of right moral power." "Parents may rely on us," read the 1857-1858 catalog, "that we will not allow any youth to remain here, if we have reason to believe him endangering his moral welfare by the formation of bad habits." Tuition was listed as forty dollars per year. The only recess during the session was Christmas day.

From the first, Lee was determined to broaden and deepen the curriculum. He agreed enthusiastically to a plan which would add five new departments to the existing six. At the first meeting of the Trustees held after his inauguration, a scheme was approved adding work in these areas: practical chemistry, including metallurgy and agricultural chemistry; practical mechanics and experimental philosophy, including mechanical drawing and architecture; applied mathematics, including astronomy and civil engineering; modern languages; and history and literature, including rhetoric, grammar, and philology. No funds were on hand to establish these chairs. But at least this was the master plan. It would be implemented as soon as possible. The Board hoped to secure some land-grant funds from the Federal Act of 1862 and to win wide private support for "General Lee's College." To build up the physical resources so that the intellectual offerings might also be increased became a consuming interest of Lee's life.

He was a strong advocate of practical, technical education, being convinced that the Reconstruction South needed it. Yet he was also a friend of the liberal arts and often expressed his lifelong regret that he had not completed his classical education before going to West Point. Without spelling out the implications of the idea, he favored a union of theory and practice, feeling that "scientific and professional studies can best be taught when surrounded by the liberalizing influence of a literary institution." Certainly he did not stress military education. This he thought the worst possible preparation for civil life. "For many years I have observed the failure in business pursuits of men who have resigned from the army," he said. "It is very rare that any one of them has achieved success."

Though he did not hesitate to speak out on various educational subjects, it is pretentious to speak of Lee's "theory" of education. He was always Aristotelian rather than Platonic: a realist, not an idealist. Today we might call Lee a pragmatist who met practical problems in a common-sense way and measured his success by the results achieved. "We must look to the rising generation for the restoration of the country," Lee wrote on March 3, 1868.

He continued to explore ways to augment this conviction. At the June, 1868 board meeting, the Trustees asked for a report on the extension of the scientific departments, to be prepared under the President's direction. In forwarding the report to the Board in March, 1869, Lee wrote: "The great object of the whole plan is to provide the facilities required by the large class of our young men, who, looking to an early entry into the practical pursuits of life, need a more direct training to this end than the usual literary courses."

In essence, the plan was to sponsor new departments of agriculture, chemistry and commerce. The first would deal with all aspects of farm management, including work on a farm owned by the College. The second would entail the use of tools practically taught—the mouth blow-pipe, for example. The third, equally precise in its orientation, would center on "commercial economy, or the administration and financial management of commercial enterprises, banks, insurance and joint stock companies, railroads, canals, ships, etc."

Engineering would also expand into three different areas: civil, mechanical, and mining. The report was quite explicit as to what students would do. An erstwhile mechanical engineer, for example, would learn how to do neat and exact working drawings of "machines, masonry, carpentry, &c.: without skill in which essential labour no one is qualified to take charge of works of construction, or superintend industrial establishments, in such a manner as is called for by the present advanced state of the arts."

Journalism was another pursuit in which the expanding

curriculum would be involved. On March 30, 1869, the faculty recommended that press scholarships be provided for young men who wanted to "make practical printing and journalism their business in life," and who were willing to work one hour each working day in a college printing plant.

The Board liked the general idea, but suggested that the actual shop work be done outside the College. The firm of Lafferty and Company in Lexington expressed a willingness to cooperate in such a venture. Thus tiny Washington College drew up plans for the first "working" school of journalism in America.

Though such a school did not take full form during Lee's lifetime, the *Southern Collegian*, a semi-monthly publication of the literary societies, did. A good deal of old Southern rhetoric carried over into its columns: "My warm Southern blood, unchilled by adversary and slavery, heated by the fires of patriotism, boiled within my veins and filled me with indignation against the ruthless invader who dared to set foot on Southern soil."

With characteristic undergraduate pride, the editors proclaimed on October 9, 1869, that, despite its poverty, Washington College was superior to either Harvard or Yale by dint of its Southern character and fine faculty. In another issue, one of the local barbers was quoted as saying: "I never saw such students. They don't shave, or smoke, or drink, or spend money. They don't do nothing but study." This caused the editor to express the belief that "our young men have in a high degree appreciated and tried to meet the duty of the hour." Articles on education were frequently featured, showing how the concern of Lee and his faculty infiltrated the student mentality. This same *Collegian* has survived nearly a century of fads and fashions, and it is still published in Lexington.

Other plans called for a summer school, closer coordination with a local private law school, "resident masterships" for outstanding young teachers, and the enlargement of faculty research. No wonder the New York *Herald* commented, in the spring of 1869, that Lee's lively new program might well "make as great an impression upon our old fogy schools and colleges as did his military tactics upon our old fogy commanders in the palmy days of the rebellion."

These were the main ideas and plans that either began or took final shape in Lee's office. The College and the South were justifiably proud of them.

But it was his treatment of human beings, not plans and papers, that most impressed his contemporaries, and posterity. On numerous occasions he stressed that *people* came first. When one of his professors invoked precedent in a discussion, Lee replied: "In dealing with young men I always respect persons, and care little for precedent." Many times he urged his colleagues not to make useless rules. "We must never make a rule that we cannot enforce," he told them.

Soon after coming to Washington College, Lee met some new students who were stopping at Rockbridge Baths before beginning their college work. He gave them a note to the proprietor of the springs which began: "My dear Major, these are some of my new boys. Please take care of them." Though he called them "Mister" to their faces, he thought of all students as his "boys." For years afterwards, to have been one of "General Lee's boys" was considered a mark of the highest distinction.

The 1860's were difficult times for anyone to oversee a

group of several hundred young men, some of whom were veterans of a brutal, bitter war. A Federal garrison was in Lexington during part of Lee's presidency. Tension was inevitable. Agitators appeared specifically to bait Lee. Race relations were strained. Lee had to quell at least two near-lynchings.

Clashes between the college students and "Toothpicks" (townspeople) were sharp. On occasions Lee made written appeals to the students or oral appeals to their leaders. When he heard that the students had organized "callithumps"—raids not unlike the "rumbles" that occur in our cities today, Lee would post instructions that were known to the students as "general orders." Years later, C. W. Hedger told of plans for a monster callithump. On the night it was to occur, Harvey McCleary, president of the Graham Literary Society, simply announced to the students: "Gentlemen, nothing doing tonight, Marse Robert says not." That was the end of it.

Such obedience sprang not only from veneration and respect, but also from the certain knowledge that the "old man" could be hard as nails when the offense demanded it. Once a student came into his office chewing tobacco. "Go out and remove that quid," Lee said, "and never appear before me again chewing tobacco." Later that day the boy returned, still chewing. Lee turned quietly to his desk, wrote a brief note and handed it to the boy with the comment that it would be posted on the bulletin board in ten minutes. It read: "Mr. _____ is dismissed from Washington College for disrespect to the President."

Once the whole student body threatened to boycott classes if they were not given more time off at Christmas. If they carried out their threat, Lee announced calmly, he would close the College.

This insistence on authority did not, however, make him an impervious administrator. He personally talked with everyone who wanted to quit, transfer or leave during term time. "He always recognized us when he met us on his strolls," former student Graham Robinson wrote, "and called us by name. It seemed remarkable to me that he was able to remember our faces and names among as many as four hundred and ten students. I also recall that his custom was to write to the parents of each boy a letter, sometimes in his own handwriting, about once a year, concerning the young man's conduct."

Numerous others vouched for Lee's memory for student names and records. In one faculty meeting he asked about a student who had fallen down in mathematics. The professor said the General must be mistaken since the boy was near the top of the class. "He got only fifty-four last month," Lee insisted. When the professor questioned this, the card was checked. An error had been made in copying the grade of eighty-four on the card. It was recorded as a fifty-four.

On another occasion, the grades of a young North Carolinian were so poor that Lee had him in and asked if a mistake had been made. The student said no, and added that he had no excuse for his failure. Because Lee knew the lad's parents personally, he explained how saddened they would be by the report. If printed in the catalog, the marks would be a permanent testimony and humiliation. "I don't know what to do," the General said. Then he tore up the report. This kind of compassion made some students admit that it was Lee, not Jehovah, whom they found themselves worshipping.

A ray of humor sometimes shone through the demanding times and job. In asking why a student was loafing, Lee liked first to commend him on the good health he was taking so much care to protect at all costs. He announced that he did not want Washington College men to injure their health, "but I wish them to come as near it as possible."

Once, when a youngster who had accumulated too many absences was called into the office, he told a tale of woe about his health. Then, realizing that he looked perfectly well, he started off on a new tack, about having left his shoes at the cobbler's. "Stop, stop!" Lee urged him. "One good reason is enough!" There was, the culprit admitted later, a twinkle in the old hero's eyes as he said it.

That General Lee's boys were cut out of the same cloth as undergraduates of all times and places can be seen by their reception of an extra required course in declamation. It was to be taught by General W. N. Pendleton, the old artillerist then serving as rector of Grace Episcopal Church. To register their protest, the boys pinned papers on the visiting orator's coat tail, applauded him excessively before he began and bombarded him with paper wads. When this was reported to Lee, the President attended the next recitation. All went well that time. But the following week, bedlam broke loose. An impromptu band blew horns outside the window. Paper balls whizzed back and forth. A dog suddenly appeared with a tin can tied to his tail. General Pendleton left the battlefield, angered and defeated, to return to the class no more.

Such incidents merely added to the *ésprit* of an expanding and expansive student body. The school that had opened in

1865 with only four professors and a few dozen students had a faculty of fourteen and a student body of one hundred and forty-six a year later. Enrollment for the 1867-1868 session opened at a record high of four hundred, and climbed to four hundred ten by June—nearly three times as many as in 1865-1866. Twenty states were represented in the student body. To match this expansion, plant and facilities were enlarged accordingly. For those who learned and those who taught, the years from 1865 to 1870 were a triumphant time at Washington College.

Lee impressed his faculty as much as he did the students. Professor Edward S. Joynes stated that "the utmost harmony and utmost energy pervaded all the departments of the college. The highest powers of both professors and students were called forth, under the fullest responsibility." "He was courteous, kind, and often rather playful in manner with the faculty," Professor William P. Johnston recalled. "We all thought he deferred entirely too much to the expression of opinion on the part of the faculty, when we would have preferred that he should simply indicate his own views or desire."

Johnston made particular note of Lee's self control. "No matter how long or fatiguing a faculty meeting might be, he always preserved an attitude in which dignity, decorum, and grace were united." That the teachers had a kind of awe for him is certain. Professor Humphreys commented that it was easy to start a conversation with Lee, but sometimes embarrassing to continue it.

If he gave them unlimited intellectual freedom, Lee did not expect his faculty men to absent themselves without permission. When one newcomer did so, Lee greeted him later with these words: "Sir, I congratulate you on your return to your friends and your duties. I was not aware of your absence until I heard it by chance." The young man was more careful about leaving the next time.

Other professors commented on the meticulous, sometimes penny-pinching, tactics which dominated Lee's office. Dr. Kirkpatrick, Professor of Moral Philosophy, came in and asked for a certain paper. The President told him where it was located. After a while Lee asked, "Did you find the paper?"

"Yes, General."

"Did you return it to the place where you found it?"

On another occasion, Professor Harris came to study a college catalog. He took up a new one, wrapped for mailing, and started to remove the wrapping. Hastily Lee intervened, saying, "Take this one, if you please," handing him an unwrapped copy.

Still there was nothing austere about the college commencement exercises, held early in June and lasting a week. "The town was crowded with visitors," the General's son Robert recalled. "My father had his house full, generally of young girls, friends of my sisters who came to assist at the final ball, the great social event connected with this college exercise. He seemed to enjoy their society as much as the young men did." The charm of General Lee's manner, the brightness of his smile and the warmth of his hospitality made a lasting impression on all those who came to the graduations.

Throughout his presidency, Lee preferred to work indirectly and anonymously for the policies he endorsed so strongly. Whenever possible he confined direct interposition to purely personal acts, and only rarely exerted presidential authority. "As a general principle," he told a young instructor, "you should not force young men to do their duty, but let them do it voluntarily and thereby develop their characters. The great mistake of my life was taking a military education."

Seldom did he mingle with students. However, on one occasion he did make a public oration to the students outside the regular commencement period. This was at a joint meeting of the Graham Philanthropic Society and the Washington Literary Society. Founded in 1809 and 1812 respectively, the societies had their own halls and were important centers of student expression and thought. Standing on the floor of the Washington Literary Society Hall, Lee told the students that it was their duty to do all they could "to add *éclat* to the exercises of the approaching commencement."

He never made a speech before the professors, preferring to listen to rather than lecture them. In his office, he was pupil as well as president. There he showed, day by day, the humility which was his true strength. One does not generally think of an office as a battlefield. Yet, for Robert E. Lee, that is just what it was. Here he had to conquer, not opposing armies, but himself. Here the man of action had to become the man of routine, to arrange papers, not battalions. Not to Chancellorsville, or Malvern Hill, or Gettysburg, must one go to see where the best of Lee manifested himself, but to that plain basement office in the college chapel. In his service, not his surging, he finally conquered.

X

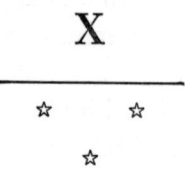

THE WEDDING

> I have no enjoyment in life but what
> I derive from my children.
> —Robert E. Lee

"I, FITZHUGH, TAKE THEE, MARY, to be my wedded wife, to have and to hold from this day forward, for better for worse, for richer for poorer, in sickness and in health. . . ."
  November 28, 1867. The Lee clan gathered in Petersburg to celebrate a wedding. With his first son at his right hand and his third son at his left, Robert E. Lee watched his second son, Fitzhugh, marry Mary Tabb Bolling.
  Standing erect and proud in the crowded Episcopal church, Lee saw the thing he cherished most in his life flourish and grow—his family.
  Underneath joyful, nuptial sounds was a note of sadness. Few could help recalling Fitzhugh's lovely first wife who died in the bleak winter of 1863 while her husband was a prisoner of war. No one could walk in Petersburg without

viewing the damage to one of the most brutally battered cities of the war. From June 1864 to April 1865, Petersburg had been the focus of the Union attack. Here the Confederates made their last effective stand. Here the line stretched until it broke. When Lee finally abandoned the city and its people, the war was over. After Petersburg, Appomattox was only a week away.

General Lee watched as his son Fitzhugh took his wedding vows. "Rooney" had always been a good boy. At Harvard he baffled and exasperated his classmate, Henry Adams; but the Adamses had been better at writing books than they had been at leading armies. Rooney received his Army commission in the far west after that, and followed his father and family into the Confederacy when the split came. Serving as a cavalry officer, Rooney was severely wounded on June 9, 1863. Afterward he was captured by the enemy and held prisoner for nine months. During this dismal period, his first wife, Charlotte Wickham, and their infant child died. For him, life was beginning all over again today.

"I, Mary, take thee, Fitzhugh, to be my wedded husband, to have and to hold from this day forward..."

Tall and imposing, Mary Bolling symbolized a generation of Southern women who stood by their men in victory and defeat and did not forget their heritage. Both sides of her family were members of the Virginia aristocracy. Like the Lees, they gave all they had to the defense of their way of life. That "way" had been buried in ashes. But they were still Tabbs and Bollings, fit partners for the Lees. The family on the bride's side rejoiced too.

"To have and to hold..."

To *have* Petersburg was one thing. To *hold* it was another. General Lee must have been looking beyond that altar, that church, and reliving his terrible nights and days there. "When our armies were in front of Petersburg," he wrote to Fitzhugh a month after the city fell, "I suffered so much in body and mind on account of the good townspeople, especially on that gloomy night when I was forced to abandon them, that I have always reverted to them in sadness and sorrow. My old feelings returned to me, as I passed well-remembered spots . . ."

Clad in a new broadcloth suit—his first since Appomattox—the General did not let his sorrow show through now. He smiled at the ten young bridesmaids and ten erect ushers. To this city of death, they brought new life. For all the Lees, and especially for their war-weary patriarch, this was a triumphant moment.

"With this ring I thee wed, in the name of the Father, and of the Son, and of the Holy Ghost."

Did the ring of the cannon pounding away from Fort Hell still resound everlastingly through Lee's massively proud head?

". . . that ye may so live together in this life, that in the world to come ye may have life everlasting. Amen."

The new daughter which the General acquired that day was no stranger. He had met her during the siege of Petersburg and had been impressed with her beauty and intelligence. When Fitzhugh told the family of the engagement in the fall of 1867, his father wrote that he had "the most pleasant recollection of her," adding: "I hope she will not delay the consummation, for I want to see her very much, and I fear she will not come to see me until then." So anxious was he to give the match his blessing that he quelled his inherent dislike of crowds and festivities, and consented to come to this memory-haunted place.

The trip was made grimmer still by a stopover in Richmond because of a Federal court subpoena in connection with Jefferson Davis' trial. Reaching Richmond, where the groom-to-be met him, Lee registered at the Exchange Hotel on November 25. That night, at Judge Ould's house, he saw President Davis for the first time since March, 1865. "He looks astonishingly well," Lee wrote to his wife. Talk between the two men was of surface matters. Each chose to leave the inner burdens concealed.

The next day Lee appeared at the Federal Building. For two hours he answered questions, mostly about military matters. All this was to establish proof and dramatize the armed rebellion against Federal authority. Undoubtedly Lee was glad to be excused from further interrogation and to leave by train the next afternoon with the large wedding party that was making the twenty-two-mile trip from Richmond to Petersburg.

En route, Lee sat silent and sad-faced, pondering all the horrors of a city of broken walls, roofless houses and dirty dilapidated streets which the name "Petersburg" conjured up. He must have seen again Fort Damnation and Fort Hell, with picket lines only seventy-five yards apart, around which the ground was as red as a butcher's block; have gazed again into the Crater, the huge irregular pit made by the Yankees' underground explosion of July 30, 1864, which had soon filled with hundreds of their own dead. Now, all around the edge, indigent Negroes would be digging out bullets, to be sold for four cents a pound as scrap metal. The names would become places again—Drewry's Bluff, Bermuda Hundred, Fort Stedman, Port Walthall Junction.

There were no names on any map that Lee dreaded more.

Petersburg, cut down in her prime, had been laid out by the same William Byrd who envisioned Richmond. Situated on the falls of the Appomattox, Petersburg was the site of the early Pocahontas settlement. In 1646, Governor William Berkeley erected Fort Henry here. Captain Peter Jones had his trading post nearby. Scores of bateaux came to the city after a canal built around the falls enabled them to move a hundred miles up-river. One of America's earliest theaters sprang up here, alongside hospitable taverns and inns. A young poet named Edgar Allan Poe had brought his thirteen-year-old bride to one of those inns. In the 1850's, Petersburg had a future. By the mid-1860's, it had only a past.

For the return of Robert E. Lee, it tried desperately to be a town of triumph, not death. At Pocahontas, a little northern suburb, a band played the "Marseillaise," always a favorite with the Rebel army. General William Mahone waited for Lee at the main station with a carriage and four prancing white horses. Shortly after arriving at the Mahone residence, Lee went over to Poplar Lawn, the Bolling residence, and presented the bride with a necklace chosen by his wife and himself. He was never too sad to show the gallantry which was his birthright.

That same inheritance made Lee enormously concerned with any marital prospects or activities in his widespread clan. Silent on many matters, he gave advice more freely than Polonius when matrimony was involved. As Robert Lee later said: "He was constantly urging his sons to take to themselves wives. With his daughters he was less pressing. Though apparently willing to have another daughter, he did not seem to long for any more sons."

Nowhere did Lee's pride show through more clearly or less attractively than when a Lee was jilted. And on one occasion he wrote his "worrying little daughter Agnes": "Sally is going to marry a widower. I think I ought to know, as she has refused my son, and I do not wish to know the man's name. I wonder if she knows how many children he has. Tell Mr. Warwick I am sorry for him. I do not know what he will do without his sweet daughter."

The General could be caustic about his own sweet—and thoroughly dominated—daughters. Of Mildred, he wrote: "She rules her brother and my nephews with an iron rod, and scatters her advice broadcast among the young men of the College ... The young mothers of Lexington ought to be extremely grateful to her for her suggestions to them as to the proper mode of rearing their children."

Why did none of his daughters every marry—or seem even to have serious suitors? One suspects that pride was a factor. From the father came the clear dictum: "Never marry unless you can do so into a family which will enable your children to feel proud of both sides of the house."

In retrospect, the Lees seem less like a family than a reigning dynasty. They were cousins to the Carters, Randolphs, Tazewells, Blands, Fitzhughs, Corbins, Nicholases, Marshalls and many others. One had to look hard to find a great Virginia manor house where the Lees were not at home. "I know no country," said George Washington, "that can produce a family, all distinguished as clever men, as the Lees." This was in 1777, a generation before the greatest of the Lees had been born.

Their luster reached back to medieval England. A Norman fighter named Reyner built a manor house called Lea (meaning meadow) amidst the rolling Shropshire hills.

Reyner de Lea was a bold and proud knight; in his wake came a family that farmed, fought and married well. The name Lea—or Lee—appeared more and more in battles and councils. One of that name commanded a British ship against the Spanish Armada. A Tudor mansion, Coton Hall, became their home base. The family's crest—a squirrel eating a nut—still hangs today on Squirrel Inn and nearby Alveley School in Shropshire.

Richard Lee, "of comely visage, vigorous spirit, and generous nature," brought the family pennant to the New World in 1640 and planted it firmly for the generations ahead. A chief aide to Governor William Berkeley, Richard married a wife who bore him eight sturdy children. By 1664, he ranked as the greatest landowner of his generation. At home on both sides of the Atlantic, he returned to his beloved Virginia home, Cobb's Hall, to die.

All four sons were educated in England; one stayed there for the rest of his life. Harold married the granddaughter of the richest *Mayflower* passenger and founded the Ditchley line of the family. Young Richard II married a Corbin, whose family had held extensive land in England for fourteen generations. He, in turn, had four sons. The last founded the famous Stratford line. Of this, Robert E. Lee was the culmination.

However, the family fortunes were at a low ebb in his childhood. His father, after leaving debtor's prison, had wandered off to the West Indies. Although he had tried desperately to get home, he had died on Cumberland Island, Georgia. His financial failure haunted his son's memory; it must have flared up when Robert E. Lee's army was defeated and his cause lost. A much greater influence on young Robert, however, was his mother, Ann Hill Carter

Lee. Despite cold, poverty, and loneliness, she held her family of five together. Her utter devotion to duty and unselfish concern for those who depended on her made an indelible impression on young Robert. Sometimes, however, Mrs. Lee could not help regretting the fate that had befallen her. A bittersweet note runs through her letters. "I may with much truth be said to live the world forgetting, by the world forgot," she wrote. Her oldest son, father and sister all died in one year. Her own health failed. But she still kept going. In these years her greatest blessing was the fifth Lee child, one she had not wanted and whom she named—after two of her brothers—Robert Edward.

No more beautiful relationship existed in Lee's entire life than that with his invalid mother. Often Robert carried her in his arms to her carriage, arranged her comfortably and, in winter, tried to shut out the winds that whistled through the old family coach. He was her nurse, her companion, her protector. No wonder she said when he left for West Point: "How can I live without Robert? He is both son and daughter to me."

If his mother dominated Lee's young years, his wife dominated most of the others. And like his mother, his wife was, for many of her years, an invalid. No single fact so influenced Lee's thinking and action during the Lexington period.

Almost two years younger than her husband, Mary Anne Randolph Custis was a thorough-going aristocrat. Her father, a grandson of Martha Washington, built Arlington, one of America's major mansions. Being the only surviving child, she inherited it. Mary Custis knew just who she was— both before and after her marriage to Robert E. Lee in 1831. She let everyone else know it, too. Unlike her husband, she never fully adjusted to the lesser station and prestige of her later years. "Life is waning away," she wrote in 1868, "and with the exception of my own immediate family, I am entirely cut off from all that I have ever known and loved in my youth. My dear old Arlington—I cannot bear to think of that used by the enemy and so little hope of my ever getting there again."

She believed in the social amenities and class distinctions that boarded on caste distinctions. A prepossessive mother, she clung tenaciously to her children—particularly her youngest son, Robert, Jr., who remained "my dear little Rob" long after he was an adult. From them, and from her husband, she received unquestioning obedience and devotion. Occasionally the General would gently chide his "Mim" for her tardiness and carelessness with money. "The Mim, the dear Mim," he once wrote to his son, "considers herself a great financier. Consult her about the expenditure of money, but do not let her take it shopping, or you will have to furnish her with an equal amount to complete her purchases."

But Lee also recognized his wife's considerable talents. She undoubtedly was quite well read for her place and time. Custis reported that she was "constantly occupied with her books, letters, knitting, and painting, for the last of which she had great talent." She wrote a memoir of her father, George Washington Parke Custis, and prepared his writings for publication. Mrs. Lee had far more fluidity and skill with words than her husband.

Yet she did not share his nobility of spirit and forgiveness. The tart remarks and complaints of her later years contrast sharply with his tolerance and optimism. She considered the Radical Republicans "cowards and base men," and thought the country "that allows such scum to rule them must fast be going to destruction, and we shall not care if we are not involved in a crash." She admitted that her indignation "cannot be controlled and I wonder how long our people can bear it."

Mrs. Lee admitted bluntly that she neither felt nor owed any allegiance to the United States, "except what is exacted by force." Nor did she feel any respect for "the military satraps who rule us." John Minor Botts of Staunton, a Union sympathizer, she called "one of the basest, meanest of men." Judge John Underwood was "one of the *blessed mementos* bequeathed to us by the 'Sainted' Lincoln, for which we are expected to be grateful; but our Southern hearts are still rebellious."

One also detects a strong note of self-pity in Mary Lee's Lexington letters. As early as June, 1866, we find her writing: "We are soon going to the Warm and Hot Springs, though I have little hope of any permanent benefit . . . Lexington has been quite gay recently with the two commencements, Washington College & the Institute; but I am unable to mix in anything that is going on & am often very sad and lonely. God knows what is best for us all, yet it often seems to me that my affliction is peculiarly trying to one of my active temperament."

Just how trying she was to her husband, no one will ever know. Being a Lee, he never said.

Even after the General was in his grave, Mrs. Lee refused to accept the defeat he had worn so gracefully. "I was ambitious enough to hope the day might come when, in a political sense at least, he might deliver our country from the thralldom that oppressed it," she wrote. "By 'our' country, I mean the South."

More tragic than the unreconciled mother were the unwed daughters, with their thin, tight-lipped faces and melancholy eyes. Mary was born in 1835, Anne in 1839, Mildred in 1846. "Precious Annie," as her father called her, died at the age of twenty-three. Agnes outlived her father only three years, dying at thirty-two. Of the Lee girls a young Washington College instructor wrote: "They don't seem to like Lexington much—think the people stiff and formal, which is very much the case. The seeming haughtiness of Agnes . . . offends the Lexingtonians." They taught classes in the local Episcopal Sunday School and joined the Reading Club. But the meetings, Agnes admitted, were "usually a small matter."

As Lee's children paced out their lusterless lives, mournful evergreens and ruined churches dotted the Tidewater area where the Lees had once flourished. A minor poet in King and Queen County struck the proper nostalgic note:

>Ah, now the time of bronze returns
>And honest cheek with flushes burns
>Cant, affectation, gloss, begone,
>Old times, old times, return return.

The Lee who returned to the Tidewater country briefly for his son's wedding knew full well that the year just ending had seen hopes dashed for swift and bloodless reconstruction. On January 7, 1867, Congress passed a resolution directing the Judiciary Committee to inquire into President Johnson's conduct and report if he were guilty of high crimes and misdemeanors. Acting with the boldness of Danton and the bitterness of Marat, Thaddeus Stevens described a President "surrounded, hampered, tangled in the meshes of his own wickedness—unfortunate, unhappy man, behold your doom." Speaking for the impeachment counsel, Senator Benjamin Butler announced that he would handle the matter like a case against any horse thief.

This same Butler would wave before Congress a nightshirt allegedly stained with Yankee blood. "Waving the bloody shirt" would become standard procedure with a certain breed of Northern politician, while his counterpart in the South also sought to inflame the people with racial hatred. A typical news item of this nature appeared in Lee's local newspaper, the Lexington *Gazette*. In a few words it catches the temper of the times: "A drunken Negro at Murfreesboro, Tenn. ran against a little girl the other day. Angered because she was in the way, he deliberately drew a revolver and blew out her brains."

Such victims of post-war brutality were presented as Southern martyrs. Other martyrs haunted Southern minds in the late 1860's: those who had fallen attempting to turn back the invaders. Again the pages of the Lexington *Gazette* furnished frequent examples. It reprinted this poetic excerpt from a paper in Jefferson County, Virginia:

> And are they really dead, our martyred slain?
> No! Dreamers! Morn shall bid them rise again
> From every vale—from every height
> On which they seemed to die for right.
> Their gallant spirits shall renew the fight
> In the land where we were dreaming.

In 1867, at least, that land would not be known officially as Virginia. A March 2, 1867, Congressional act divided the ex-Confederacy into five military districts, of which Virginia was the first. Military officers exerted interim power.

Adult males, regardless of color and not disenfranchised by participating in rebellion, were allowed to vote for delegates to a constitutional convention. When a majority of qualified persons had ratified such a constitution, when the national Congress had approved it, and when the military district had ratified the Fourteenth Amendment to the national Constitution, then the territory could be readmitted into the Union as a state. In short, Congress assumed complete responsibility for Reconstruction.

Reading of these measures, General Lee made no comment. But his wife did, in a letter to a Tidewater friend. "How long, O Lord?" she asked, "how long?"

If Lee would not permit himself to make any public statement about the course of events or be drawn into the political maelstrom, he did write candidly of this action in several private letters. He wrote to General Dabney Maury suggesting that the best be made of a bad situation. "The question is, shall the members of the convention be selected from the best available men in the State, or the worst?" In a second letter to a Petersburg friend, he pointed out that whatever was done "can be improved as opportunity offers." The dominant party would not reign forever, he reminded his son Fitzhugh in February, 1867, "and truth and justice will at last prevail." The fact that General Lee could continue to believe in happy endings, no matter how unhappy the events preceding, was the secret of his incredible equanimity. "The time is not distant," he wrote to Robert, "when the angry cloud will be lifted from our horizon and the sun in his pristine brightness again shine forth."

Meanwhile, there were dark moments. On March 22, 1867, one occurred in Lexington itself. Five of General

Lee's students—one of them carrying a pistol—went to a rally of the town Negroes. Words, threats, blows followed, and only quick action on the part of the other students prevented the pistol from coming into play. On such occasions President Lee acted swiftly and decisively. He became General Lee once again. The pistol-bearer was quickly expelled, his accomplices reprimanded. Thus further action on the part of the assistant superintendent of the Freedman's Bureau was averted. Still, the episode showed the explosive quality of Southern life, even in isolated villages; and it kept Lee constantly on guard, lest any such spark set off a bonfire in which he, and through him all the South, might become involved.

Not all the news was gloomy, however. In the spring of 1867, President Jefferson Davis was released on bail, to Lee's great satisfaction. "Your release has lifted a load from my heart which I have not words to tell . . . That the rest of your days may be triumphantly happy is the sincere and earnest wish of your most obedient, faithful friend and servant." Underneath the stilted phrases we detect the deep loyalty which always remained one of Lee's most attractive features.

The summer had gone pleasantly enough, but the General's spirits were not high when the fall term began. Sturdy and robust throughout the war, he was increasingly plagued by aches and pains after 1865. "I am still so feeble," he admitted to Rooney on September 20, "that I cannot attend to the pressing business connected with the College." Yet he did not hesitate, two months later, to take time off for Rooney's wedding. By now, his children and students had become the fulcrum which operated his whole life. Visiting Petersburg in the fall of 1867 was a mandate.

Two days after the wedding, General Lee returned to Richmond for short visits with friends. On December 2, he went down his beloved James River to visit the Harrisons at Brandon and the Wickhams at Hickory Hill. Amongst his "own people," he always blossomed. The marriage of Custis pleased him very much, as did the ability of eastern Virginians to recover from the terrible war. After his longest absence from Lexington since assuming the presidency, he started back on December 6 in unusually high spirits. The oncoming Christmas season would see the family united in a festive mood. After years in the saddle, he had found peace on earth, in the valley of Virginia.

XI

☆ ☆
☆

THE LONG WINTER

> Who shall hold in behometh?
> Who bridle leviathan?
> —Walt Whitman

Back with his unwed daughters and ailing wife, Lee's health began to decline with an alarming rapidity. The 1868 photographs show a man who looks ten, not three years, older than the power-packed figure who posed for Matthew Brady in 1865. Strong and athletic then, he had shown no effects of the one serious illness he suffered during the war—an "inflammation of the heart-sac" in the spring of 1863. Ever since Appomattox, however, he had referred to trouble which was described variously as rheumatism, lumbago or sciatica. More and more susceptible to colds and aches after 1867, the General talked constantly of growing old and of having only a little while longer to live. Privately his friends said that he was having trouble "about the heart" and noted that he looked weary and haggard. Lee admitted to frequent pains while walking, especially "along the breastbone." All indications point to an inadequately diagnosed heart condition.

He was in no shape to take on a new series of hard blows that befell him. In February 1868, the Senate debated the circumstances surrounding his resignation from the United States Army before the Civil War. This proved to be one of the most agonizing events of his life. In a hassle over the seating of Philip F. Thomas of Maryland, Senator Simon Cameron, Lincoln's Secretary of War in 1861, claimed that Lee had agreed to take command of the Union Army and had said he would return to Virginia only to settle his business and return. "He deserted under false pretenses," Cameron concluded. Although Maryland's senior senator, Reverdy Johnson, attempted to deny this story, he was able neither to make Cameron recant nor get Thomas seated.

Usually loath to answer accusations, Lee regarded this attack as a blow at his integrity. He wrote to Senator Johnson, giving his version of the resignation. "I never intimated to any one that I desired the command of the United States Army," Lee wrote, "I declined the offer Mr. Francis Preston Blair made me, to take command of the army that was to be brought into the field ... These are the simple facts of the case, and they show that Mr. Cameron has been misinformed." This was among the strongest letters Lee ever wrote; its emotional undercurrent makes it one of his most memorable.

During the same bleak February when he was trying to answer Cameron, the most serious charges made against the College during Lee's presidency were beginning to take form in Lexington. A nasty local incident known as the "Johnston affair" was twisted and inflated until it had national implications. E. C. Johnston was a Yankee carpetbagger who moved to Lexington in 1867 as an agent of the American Missionary Association. Having worked for a while setting up a Negro school, he became a storekeeper. He was no more popular with the white natives than one would expect under the circumstances; besides, he was belligerent enough to carry a pistol about town, which did not help matters. After a row with local people at an ice-skating party on February 4, Johnston drew the pistol and threatened to use it on one of his defamers, a lad whose age was later estimated as low as twelve and as high as seventeen. As a result, Johnston was driven from the ice, bruised and infuriated. He was able to transform the confused incident into a *cause célèbre*.

First he went to Lexington's mayor, J. M. Ruff, demanding revenge and protection. Since Johnston could name no assailants, Ruff would do nothing—he could not control townspeople and college students to accommodate carpetbaggers. More angry than ever, Johnston then took the matter to the military authorities. The bloodthirsty story he told Brigadier General Douglas Frazer was passed on to Major General O. B. Willcox whose headquarters was in Lynchburg. Willcox rushed to Lexington. The gauntlet was down.

Having looked into the matter, Willcox went to Lee and named three students who were allegedly involved. Without waiting for general faculty action, Lee talked to the three boys, directed one to withdraw immediately, and wrote the parents of another to call him home. The third student, an observer but not a participant, asked for and received permission to withdraw, too, and did so. All this Lee made known to Willcox before the latter left town. Reporting officially that he saw "no signs of any disposition to screen disturbers of the peace," the investigating Federal then went back to Lynchburg.

After that, Johnston, realizing that he would be safer elsewhere, planned to move his business across the mountain to Covington. Before going, he received other taunts and visits from irate townspeople. Since he could no longer interest the Northern army in his predicament, Johnston decided to carry his case to the Northern press.

If he had wanted to choose the most disruptive moment, he could not have found a better time. That very month Washington College had launched its campaign for support in New York City. In the main hall of Cooper Institute, a March 3 rally was planned. Its sponsors hoped it would mark a turning point not only in the history of Washington College, but of Southern education as well. Such prominent men as Henry Ward Beecher, Peter Cooper, Horace Greeley and Governor Reuben E. Fenton had agreed to help. Professor Roswell Hitchcock of the Union Theological Seminary had prepared a speech describing Robert E. Lee as a gentleman, patriot and scholar, entitled to all honor. But at this very moment, E. C. Johnston gave his alarming version of the state of affairs in Lexington, Virginia.

The New York *Independent* was his chief vehicle. The more prominent *New York Times* and *Tribune* soon became involved as well. The *Independent* not only dramatized this particular episode, but made up new ones of its own. When Lee had resigned from the Union Army, according to the *Independent*, he not only promised to return, but carried off the maps of Washington's defenses to boot. (This version was later reprinted by *Harper's Weekly*.) "We have also been reminded of the fact," the *Independent* continued, "that slaves found on Lee's plantation at Arlington averred that he had treated them with atrocious cruelty."

Suddenly Lee's whole academic program and the financial campaign his college had undertaken were in jeopardy. "Is *this* the sort of college to which the Christian loyalists of the North should make contributions?" the *Independent* asked. A short time later, the newspaper carried a letter signed by "A Resident of Lexington." It made this unequivocal charge: "I feel it my duty to show the philanthropists of the North the animus of the institution to which they are contributing. The Lexington professors are, without a single exception, thoroughly rebel in sentiment, and act accordingly. No student can remain in the College who is not a rebel."

The journalistic appeal of such stories in a North constantly reminded that Dixie had got off too easily was tremendous. Chicago papers now lashed out at Lee as if he were Lucifer leading the rebel hosts. The Boston *Traveler* pronounced Washington College "lawless" and denounced Lee's presidency. The Yale College paper rebuked its sister institution in the South. In this instance, Lee wrote personally to set the record straight. But just how many charges went unanswered, in word and print, no one can say. If E. C. Johnston wanted revenge, he certainly got it. The embarrassment and concern caused to Lee and others in Lexington cannot be measured. What the carpetbagger could not do with his pistol was done for him by printer's ink.

Lee had pistol troubles, too. Later that spring, the son of Judge Brockenbrough was assailed and shot by a Negro near the grounds of Washington College. Too young to be in college himself, Francis Brockenbrough had two brothers there. When word of the incident reached the students, they did not wait for the law to take over. Capturing Caesar, the Negro involved, they put a rope around his neck and dragged him to the courthouse square. Already word had reached poor whites in the county. They headed for the courthouse, too, shouting, "Lynch him!"

As soon as he heard the news, Lee hurried to the scene. Quietly he ordered the students to turn Caesar over to the authorities and to go back to their rooms. Unfortunately, young Brockenbrough's condition grew worse that night. If he died, several students were heard to say they intended to break into the jail and string up Caesar. This rumor reached Lieutenant Jacob Wagner, the local military commissioner. He requested troops from General Willcox in Lynchburg. A company of Yankees arrived quickly; Wagner thought they were insufficient and requested more. The troops patrolled the streets with fixed bayonets. At any minute the whole situation might explode. Once again the principles Lee advocated were endangered by a fortuitous incident.

As always, he worked out the problem with as little show of power as possible. Issuing no official statements or charges, he contacted student leaders, many of whom were former Confederate soldiers. He told them that there must be no violence. They gave him their word that none would occur so far as the students were concerned.

Francis Brockenbrough recovered. The Federals returned to Lynchburg, and Caesar was given a two-year sentence at the November term of the circuit court. The crisis was over.

Merely listing harrowing episodes such as these three—

and there were others—does not show why 1868 was such a trying time for Robert E. Lee. Basically the matter was psychological. He grew tired of playing demigod. Thrust suddenly into a heroic role after a relatively unheroic career before the Civil War, he had acted his part in battle because he believed in the fight and in the cause. He did not mind being the White Knight so long as there was a military crusade to be won. All this changed after Appomattox. His personal ambitions and fortunes crushed, Lee wanted to finish his life in quiet dignity and privacy. But his people, having no other heroes to take his place, would not let him abdicate. The obscure college, which he had sought out as a refuge, became famous. The more he was idolized, the more Lee agonized. For his dilemma, there was no easy answer.

He could not retreat now. Whatever the fate of Washington College, he would have to share it. Spartan devotion was the sole honorable course open to him.

"Work is what we now require," he wrote his brother as the long winter drew to an end, "work by everybody and work especially by *white* hands. Labor and economy will carry us through ... By this course the good old times of former days which you speak of will return again. We may not see them but our children will, and we will live over again in them."

Some have accused Robert E. Lee of being a sentimentalist. He was not. He knew the "good old days" were gone. If he continued to symbolize them for others, he himself was far too realistic to dramatize them in his own mind.

Lee accepted his conclusion; he did not try to rationalize it. The austerity to which he and his family were reduced never appealed to him. Obviously he preferred fine surroundings, clothing and furniture. He was a Cavalier, not a

Puritan. But dwelling with the Scotch-Irish and in a valley ravaged by civil war, he accepted the consequences. Instead of sipping fine brandy after dinner, as his ancestors had done in Tidewater, he sat quietly beside Mrs. Lee, who passed her evening hours mending her family's underclothing.

Thus, the Lee who epitomized glory in 1864 became the embodiment of submission in 1868. To those who saw him at a distance, the change was painless. But not to those who looked closer. Writing later in the *Confederate Veteran*, one of Lee's students, John B. Collyar, made this comment: "I never saw a sadder expression than General Lee carried during the entire time I was at Washington College. It looked as if the sorrow of a whole nation had collected in his countenance, and as if he was bearing the grief of his whole people."

Though he did not follow national affairs closely, Lee could not help observing the deterioration of public morality in the late 1860's. The word "fraud" took on a new meaning. A final audit showed, for example, that over seventeen million dollars of Federal government wartime contracts worth fifty million had been tinged with fraud. But if Yankee pockets bulged with war profits in 1865, these were as nothing compared to the post-war profits made in the Gilded Age. The same General Grant who had handled his army so well became a political pawn for unscrupulous men. Abuses of those years are too well known to require retelling here. The essential point is that this was the backdrop against which Robert E. Lee and the other Southern aristocrats had to live out their lives.

In 1868, South Carolina's Wade Hampton, "Giant in Gray," declared himself bankrupt. The proud Hamptons had served as the political Warwicks among cotton planters.

Before secession, Wade Hampton ruled paternalistically over a kingdom of three thousand slaves. Now, destroyed by personal debts of over a million dollars, he symbolized —with Lee—the old patrician civilization that could not survive.

A few intellectuals fought on. Alexander Stephens completed his *Constitutional View of the Late War between the States*, in which he contended that slavery was only "a drop in the ocean compared with other considerations involved in the issue." George Fitzhugh labored to graft a new philosophy of industrial monopoly onto the old aristocratic agrarian ideas. They were, in effect, merely writing the Confederacy's epitaph.

Under the circumstances, many Southern politicians came —some more quickly than others—to play the inevitable game of accommodation. By midsummer 1868, seven ex-Confederate states—Alabama, Arkansas, Florida, Georgia, Louisiana, North Carolina and South Carolina—had organized their governments and swallowed the bitter pill of the Fourteenth Amendment. Having agreed that Negro suffrage would "forever remain a part of their fundamental laws," they had been readmitted to the Union. Virginia, still recalling her nicknames, "Old Dominion" and "Mother of States," stayed out. Thus she missed an opportunity to regain some of her former power.

When reality becomes unbearable, mythology takes over. By 1868, defeat and despair had sunk into Southern pores, saturated Southern thinking and developed a new mythology. Post-war Dixie would rest on a three-legged stool: white supremacy, anti-intellectualism, and nostalgia. Henry Timrod, best Southern poet of the generation, wrote:

> Sleep sweetly in your humble graves,
> Sleep, martyrs of a fallen cause;
> Though yet no marble column craves
> The pilgrim here to pause.

Lee's most nostalgic moments came during his visits to the spas and springs in western Virginia: White Sulphur Springs, Hot Springs, Warm Springs, Rockbridge Alum Springs. Famous before the war, they continued even in Reconstruction to reflect the glow of the aristocratic way of life. Convinced that taking the waters helped his chronically sick wife, who had sustained a pelvic infection in childbirth and afterward developed a severe case of general arthritis, Lee visited the springs frequently in his final years. Like Ponce de Leon, he hoped that somehow the health and vitality that was leaving his wife and himself could be restored by the magic bubbling waters.

Opened only in 1856, the nearby Rockbridge Alum Springs received more visits from the Lees than any other. Less than twenty miles northwest of Lexington, they were accessible in a day. John Jordan, Jr., son of the architect of pre-war Washington Hall and the V. M. I. barracks, built the Rockbridge spa. Patronized by those who were more anxious for quiet than gaiety, this spa was ideal for Mrs. Lee. By building a wall around several springs, a pool of clear invigorating water had been formed. Dr. Samuel Brown Morrison, ex-Confederate surgeon, was on duty.

In addition to the main hotel, there were cottages, lawns, and a Lovers' Lookout Links for golfers. Elaborate medical analyses, prepared in the manner of the time, showed that users of the water could expect relief of ailments ranging from torpid liver to scrofula. Always the prescription was the same: drink all you can stand during the day, commencing one hour after each meal. Judging from the number of visits various Lees paid to the Alum during the 1860's, they consumed thousands of glasses in their pursuit of better health.

However, the Lees enjoyed most of all the Greenbrier, White Sulphur Springs. To go there, they would take the stage to Goshen, the train to Covington, and the carriage to the springs just across the new state line of West Virginia. The hotel was a rambling, neo-classical structure, with a wide veranda and Grecian columns, surrounded by several rows of small cottages. The Lees' preference was the Harrison Cottage in Baltimore Row. Promenading up and down through the parlors, preserving the amenities for which the Old South had been famed, the people who went to the springs enjoyed their special world, as have many before and since. The arrival of General Lee presented a problem that one lady, Christiana Bond, discussed in her diary: "There was some hurried consultation as to how he should be received. Some honor, of course, must be shown him, but would applause embarrass him? Before the question could be answered, Lee entered. There was a moment's hush. Then, as if by common impulse, every one rose and remained silent and standing until he took a seat."

On one Lee visit, the story spread that General Grant was about to visit Greenbrier, too. A young girl was bold enough to ask General Lee what he would do in that event.

"If General Grant comes, I shall welcome him to my home, show him all the courtesy which is due from one gentleman to another, and try to do everything in my power to make his stay here agreeable."

But Grant had other things to do than to promenade

around the Virginia Springs. He had set his sights on the White House. In a wartime generation, his appeal was irresistible. Grant carried twenty-six of the thirty-four states in the 1868 elections. That Christmas the outgoing president, Andrew Johnson, issued a universal amnesty including practically all former Confederates—including Robert E. Lee. The graying rebel was pleased, but not jubilant, at the news. He was still on parole, and would be until he died. Whatever pardon was or was not in store for him depended on a higher force than the Federal government.

XII

THE STROLL

> Walk while ye have the light
> lest darkness come upon you.
> —Saint John

HAD YOU VISITED Lexington, Virginia, in the spring of 1869, you might have seen a stiff, straight old man leave his new house at Washington College and stroll down into the village. Everything about him—his bearing, glance, manner and dress—would have indicated that he was no ordinary person. An aura set him apart. You might have guessed this was Robert E. Lee.

The house he built, on the site of the town's early ice house, was one of his last major achievements. A two-story structure with a large central hall and four rooms topped by four more, it was the house of an engineer, not that of an architect. Although he did not approve of the large outlay—about fifteen thousand dollars, he accepted the expenditure in the spirit which the Board intended, and followed every detail of the construction throughout 1868 and 1869. "I had intended to get down to your farm this spring," he wrote his son Robert in March, 1869, "but I fear the dilatoriness of the workmen in finishing the house, and the necessity of my attending to it, getting the grounds inclosed, and preparing the garden will prevent me. I shall also have to superintend the moving." The keys were presented to him in a formal ceremony on May 31, 1869. All those who inspected the new home were impressed.

Around two thirds of the house was a spacious porch to accommodate Mrs. Lee's wheelchair. Here she would sit for hours with "Mrs. Ruffner," her much-petted cat. In style the house was victorian with a Georgian echo. Perfectly symmetrical in front, it was embellished with various wooden ornaments. Four large chimneys and inside wooden blinds reminded one of Stratford, Lee's birthplace. The outside walls were made of three layers of brick. An air space between the inner and outer walls provided primitive air conditioning. The whole structure had a fortress-like appearance befitting the home of a general.

Since she could not mount stairs, Mrs. Lee's room was on the first floor. A ramp allowed her to wheel out to the connecting greenhouse. The General's own favorite spot was the bay window in the dining room; from there he could look out over the college campus. Behind the house were two large cisterns, holding the water supply.

Close by was Traveller's stable, complete with Palladian windows and shutters. The cow-house, woodshed and garden shed were also planned by the meticulous and thorough General Lee. Certainly this was not like the grand manor houses he had known earlier in his life, but it was solid, honest and functional. He was obviously pleased with it.

Only a few hundred yards from the Episcopal church and a few blocks from the town, the house was conveniently located. More than that, it anchored him to the community in a way that had not been possible before. With the house's foundation, Lee's roots went down into Rockbridge County soil. This was his home, and that of his children.

The town into which he often strolled in 1869 had made enormous strides forward since his arrival. Any reader of the Lexington *Gazette* could tell this. The bitter, hysterical note had disappeared from the news columns. The wonders of the West took precedent over the woes of the South. Out West, the cattle business was booming, and new brands were appearing all over the Texas range. Two weeks before Lee accepted the keys to his new house, the Central Pacific linked up with the Union Pacific at Promontory Point, Utah. Leland Stanford himself drove in the last solid gold spike with a silver hammer. The same month Major J. W. Powell and nine men risked their lives going down the Colorado River through the gorge of the Grand Canyon. A steamboat named the *Robert E. Lee* was plying the Mississippi between New Orleans and St. Louis in the incredible time of only four days. Men were talking about racing her against the *Natchez*. P. T. Barnum was about to start touring with "The Greatest Show on Earth." The Southwest provided its own particular kind of entertainment, with the James boys, the Daltons and Billy the Kid playing leading roles.

In the South some of the old gay spirit returned. By 1869, plans were underway to revive Mardi Gras parades in New Orleans. That same year, five Southern cities organized the Alabama Association of Base Ball Players.

In Lexington, too, business was thriving; luxury items

were again available. "Gentlemen who wish to wear good clothes" could go to James Compton's for "plain and fancy cashmeres, linen drills and ducks, and Marseilles vestings." Their wives would find there "white, colored, and figured piqué, plain and fancy percales, figured jaconets and organdies." S. P. McClain was prepared to make "boots, shoes, gaiters, &c., to order in the best manner," while several millinery shops invited ladies to see their new styles. J. P. Rhodes ran a "first class bakery" and dispatched his bread wagon daily. Railroads, packet boats and stage lines vied for business. Ads for patent medicines and false teeth competed for space with such items as whiskies, china and pianos. Baker & Lewis were ready to supply "Masser's Five minutes ice cream freezers, English Chow Chows, Liquid Rennet, Sapolia for polishing silverware, Sea Moss Farine and Hecker's Farina for Blanc Manges, &c." The lean years were over.

Of the unofficial life of the college president who went strolling through this town, little is known. For one thing, Lee wrote nothing himself. We knew his external movements but not his inner thoughts. He was held in such veneration by his neighbors that they did not always treat him as a mortal. Plainly, Robert E. Lee was a paragon. Only occasionally did his contemporaries put aside the platitudes and show us the man. One who did was Mrs. Margaret J. Preston. Her diary tells us more than a dozen pretentious, cliché-ridden chronicles. At one College commencement, Mrs. Preston recalled, a little lad of four went wandering up the aisles, looking for his parents. General Lee noticed the child, beckoned him over to the platform, and smiled as he made his way among the dignitaries. Leaning his head against Lee's leg, the child fell asleep, his protector's arm around him. When it was time for Lee to officiate, he did so without rising from his seat. He did not want to disturb the tired little boy.

Another day the General and a friend were riding out of town when a miller with a five-syllable German name came out of his mill to shake his idol's hand. Months passed before the two met again. Though he passed the mill frequently, Lee's riding companion had forgotten the miller's name, but Lee rode up to the workman, spoke his name clearly and distinctly, and recalled the war episode they had discussed at the earlier meeting.

Once Lee found himself in a living room with two boys playing marbles on the carpet. An argument arose. They began wrestling. Unable to persuade them to stop, Lee would not allow himself to intervene physically. "I remonstrated, I commanded," he later told Mrs. Preston. "But they were like two fierce mastiffs, and never in my military career had I to own myself so absolutely defeated. I retired beaten from the field, and let the little fellows fight it out."

If he gave in to small boys, Lee remembered how heroically his own soldier lads fought vastly superior forces in the last days of the war. Occasionally he and Mrs. Lee would relive together those awful months. One night, sitting on her porch, she recalled the difference between the appearance of the gaunt, ragged Rebels who evacuated Richmond and the superbly equipped Federals who took it over. Pacing the floor, Lee looked at her with a suddenly animated face. "But ah, Mistress Lee," he said, with a ring in his voice, "we gave them some hard knocks, for all of our rags!"

The student episode which best sums up his character involved a sophomore who was called to Lee's office because of inattention to his work.

"If you do not improve, you will fail your work," Lee pointed out.

"But General, *you* were a failure," the young man replied brashly.

"Yes. But let us hope you will be more fortunate than I," Lee replied quietly.

Lee had no "best" friend in Lexington, although he had many acquaintances and confidants. The closest of these was his pastor and former chief of artillery, the Reverend William Nelson Pendleton.

Two years younger than Lee, Pendleton was also a West Point graduate and faculty member before leaving the army for the Episcopal priesthood. In 1839, he founded, near Alexandria, Virginia, the Episcopal High School. He was principal there for many years. When war came, Pendleton was rector of Lexington's Grace Church. Entering the fight, his skill with artillery soon won him fame and his battle command—"Lord have mercy on their souls: fire!" —became part of the Confederate legend. Returning to Lexington on rain-soaked Good Friday, April 14, 1865, the fighting parson was broken in body but not in spirit. On Easter morning he baptized his grandson and invited the family to a feast made possible by gifts from a Lynchburg lady—two uncooked beef tongues and a box of sardines. Turning to the plough, Pendleton assisted by his daughters, planted a crop of corn. He was a rough-clad, mud-stained, God-fearing man, who not only endured, but triumphed.

In 1868, Pendleton set out to enlarge or rebuild his tiny church. Despite his feelings toward the Union, he solicited money from Northerners. "Our people are crippled in means and unable to do more than struggle for bare subsistence," he wrote to Bishop Horatio Potter of New York. "The actual state of affairs, could you see it, would send a shudder through your soul."

Lee was his constant supporter and companion in Lexington. Both of them had to engage continuously in the unhappy task of fund-raising. "This wandering about as a beggar is a grief my friends can hardly appreciate," Pendleton wrote to his wife the year Lee died. Outliving Lee by thirteen years, Pendleton never preached in the new church he worked so hard to build. The first service held in it was his funeral.

Another companion of Lee and the recipient of many of his informal visits, was General Francis H. Smith, superintendent of the Virginia Military Institute from 1839 to 1889. Lee and Smith were both from Tidewater families, both graduates of West Point, both professional soldiers and life-long devotees of Virginia. Both gave all their resources to the Confederacy, and their remaining energies to Southern education after the battles were lost.

Smith's job in revitalizing V. M. I. was, if anything, more difficult than Lee's at Washington College. The Institute was almost totally destroyed by General David Hunter's raid, and the school was denied privileges extended to others during Reconstruction. Nevertheless, by 1867, two companies totaling two hundred and eighty men were under training at V. M. I. Though Lee frequently discussed educational matters with Smith, he avoided showing any militaristic leanings. Whenever the two marched in local parades, Lee took pains to march out of step, thus playing down any military connotations.

Lee's friends, however, were often far humbler people. One of these was an ex-private who had come to Lexington after the war to be General Lee's photographer. Born in the Shenandoah Valley in 1841, captured by the Yankees the day Stonewall Jackson was shot, Michael Miley spent the last years of the struggle in a prison camp. Weighing less than a hundred pounds when released, he walked home, studied photography with a Lynchburg man and set up his shop in Lexington. A person of great sensitivity, Miley's photographs of the local landscape are full of spirituality and hope.

However, he is best known for his pictures of Lee and his family. Usually unsympathetic with newsmen and photographers, Lee felt a warm attachment to Miley and visited his studio frequently. To this shy, competent young man he brought such famous clients as President Davis, General Beauregard and General Early. He requested that Miley take his picture mounted on Traveller, one of the few times after Appomattox that Lee donned his Confederate uniform.

Miley idolized his patron, saying: "I consider him the greatest man that ever lived." Only twenty-nine years old when Lee died in 1870, Miley took the picture of the funeral which is reprinted in this volume.

Yet despite his constant kindness to all around him, few Lexingtonians broke through the aura around Lee. On his own faculty, Professor J. J. White was as close to Lee as any man. Frequently they took long rides together into the countryside. Once they had to spend the night in a farmhouse with one vacant bed. The thought of sharing this with Lee was outlandish: "I would as soon have thought of sleeping with the Archangel Gabriel as with the General!" White admitted. Then he added wistfully: "No man was great enough to be intimate with General Lee." In the final analysis, this isolation from others must have been the heaviest cross Robert E. Lee had to bear.

The place of both the living and the dead Stonewall Jackson in Lee's life has caused much speculation. Were they kindred souls? If so, was the grave of Jackson in Lexington one of the magnets that pulled Lee there? A popular lithograph of the time, one by A. J. Völck, is labeled "Lee Kneeling at the Grave of Jackson." Their wartime rapport and mutual admiration is well documented. But during the post-war years, Lee said little and wrote nothing about his "right arm." No visits by Lee to Jackson's grave are mentioned in local newspapers or diaries. Here again, only Lee knew Lee's thoughts.

Jackson and Lincoln were gone, but Lee's great military opponent, U. S. Grant, still lived. What might have been the most dramatic and meaningful event of Lee's last years took place in the spring of 1869. This was the meeting of Lee and President Grant in the White House on May 1, 1869. It was suggested by General Grant and arranged by Mr. and Mrs. Tagart, Baltimore friends of General Lee. Accompanied by the Tagarts, Lee drove from Baltimore to the White House about eleven that morning and introduced himself to Grant's secretary, Robert M. Douglas. John L. Motley, who witnessed the meeting, said that both men were simple and dignified. The Generals shook hands. Grant invited Lee to sit down. Comments about contemporary matters were made. Grant later recalled that they had talked of building railroads and that he had said: "You and I, General, have had more to do with destroying railroads than building them." Lee did not smile and made no other references to past events.

In short, what could have been an important conference turned out to be just a social call. Lee never saw Grant again after he left his office that day.

Episodes such as this have provided Lee's critics with one of the few tenable grounds for criticism. In *The Turning Stream*, Duncan Aikman asserts that Lee lacked the open and winning personality that might have allowed his genius full sway. Instinctively he hid behind a mask. "The perfection of Lee becomes somewhat oppressive," J. K. Hosmer writes in *The Appeal to Arms*. "One would welcome the discovery of a shortcoming in him, as redeeming him to humanity."

If any of Lee's Lexington neighbors felt this way, they did not say so. In this regnant figure they saw the drama of their people and the fame of their community. Lee's coming to their village was good fortune beyond compare. Their prevailing attitude toward him was gratitude.

Always insisting that his neighbors made too much over an old rebel, Lee returned their warm regards. He tried to be a helpful citizen, and supported generously local philanthropies such as soldiers' relief, libraries and the Bible Society. And, too, he broke his rule of non-involvement in political and economic affairs by actively supporting the scheme to bring a railroad to Lexington.

In April, 1869, he went to Baltimore to present a petition to the Mayor and City Council urging them to sponsor a railroad to the valley of Virginia, "which in climate, soil, minerals, and well distributed and continuous water power is believed not to be excelled in native wealth by any region of equal extent of this continent." Lee also sang the praises of "the numerous mineral springs, the literary institutions of Lexington, the famous Natural Bridge of Rockbridge, and the picturesque scenery." It was the closest thing to a promotional scheme in which General Lee was ever involved.

No wonder the people of Lexington respected the gray-haired man who strolled through their town. Coming as an outsider, he did not scorn their poverty and plain ways. He put away his Cavalier manner and inheritance. He wanted to belong, and they accepted him. By the time of his death, Robert E. Lee was no general in exile. He was a citizen around whom both the life of the college and of the community pivoted.

Once this became true, the "honeymoon period" and novelty of his job was over. Now he would have to take the knocks with the smiles, just like everyone else. The winter of 1868, we have seen, had its quota of knocks. In every instance Lee acted decisively and maturely to mend the situation as best he could. He did not sentimentalize over "his boys" if their dismissal was the lesser of several evils; he just went ahead and expelled them. He was not anxious that his decisions be popular, but they must be just.

The inability of his beloved Virginia to provide much-needed leadership to the South, as she had done so often earlier, must have grieved Lee deeply. Rather than leading her sister states back into the Union, Virginia stayed in the abyss while they went forward, thus refuting in fact what Lee claimed in theory. Precisely at this point of his life, we see what a real champion Robert E. Lee was. He did not despair because his hopes turned out to be futile. He just gritted his teeth and kept going.

XIII

THE TREK

> In peace there's nothing so becomes a man
> As modest stillness and humility.
> —Shakespeare

Early in 1870, Lee made his longest post-war trek. Undertaken to improve his waning health, it became a sort of triumphant procession. The vanquished general was hailed as few conquerors in history have been. He saw—finally and fully—just what he meant to the Southern people. In their hearts he had replaced his own idol, George Washington.

The trip began in late March, lasted two months and covered almost two thousand miles. Despite the wide acclaim, the venture had about it a bittersweet taste. The warm sunlight was that of a brief Indian summer. Standing amidst the bright rays, Lee knew that the unending winter would soon come.

Trudging southward to cheat death, Lee's special wish was to visit two family graves—his daughter Annie's and that of his father, "Light-Horse Harry." He wrote to his son Fitzhugh on March 22, 1870, "If I am to visit both graves, I have no time to lose. I wish to witness Annie's quiet sleep . . . and to feel that her pure spirit is waiting in bliss in the land of the blessed." The deep wound inflicted by her premature death never healed.

As for the medicinal benefits to be derived, he was skeptical. On several occasions he regretted having left home. "Doctors do not know everything," he wrote to Mildred just before embarking, "and yet I have often had to do what I was told, without any benefit to myself, and I shall have to do it again." He not only doubted the omniscience of his doctors, but came as close as he ever did in his life to complaining about carrying out an order. Lee habitually did what he was told, often without personal benefit, but he almost never fussed about doing so. His chronic pain, and the varying opinions among the many doctors who thumped on him, were partly to blame. Perhaps, too, he had a premonition that, instead of prolonging his life, the trip would shorten it.

When the time came to depart, he did not falter. On Thursday afternoon, March 24, he and his daughter Agnes who was to serve as his nurse went across town to the river and boarded the Lynchburg packet boat. The overnight boat trip to Lynchburg and the dusty train ride to Richmond Lee found "very trying." Moving into the Exchange and Ballard House, the General was soon besieged by numerous visitors. One of them, John Stewart, had provided the Richmond home to which he had come after Appomattox. "Many of my northern friends have called on me," Lee wrote his wife. "They like to see what is going on." Like it or not, Lee had to see them. He did not have to visit the floor of the Virginia Senate, however, and declined that invitation. Not to be turned away were a trio of doctors—Huston, McCaw, and Cunningham—who subjected him to a long examination. "I feel a little better than when I left Lexington," he wrote, "certainly stronger, but am a little feverish."

For exercise he strolled across the overhead bridge connecting the two wings of the hotel. Pacing the short distance, he saw the man whom the exasperated Yankees never seemed able to spot—Colonel John Mosby. That sharp-eyed ranger saw Lee, too, and recorded later: "The General was pale and haggard, and did not look like the Apollo I had known in the army." Mosby went to Lee's room to chat of many things—but not of the war. As he left the hotel, he unexpectedly met one of Lee's few outspoken Confederate critics, General George Pickett. If Mosby would return with him, he, too, would make a courtesy call, Pickett said, but he did not want to be alone with Lee.

The two men returned. The resulting meeting was tense and trying. There was iciness in Lee's words and manners, though no show of rudeness. Mosby beat a hasty retreat, followed closely by Pickett. Outside, Pickett railed against "that old man who had my division massacred at Gettysburg." Lee never wrote or spoke of their meeting. Always, in the final analysis, silence was his most powerful weapon.

Lee seldom missed a Sunday service, but he did not attend on March 27. "I was afraid to go," he wrote his wife. "The day is unfavourable, and I should see so many of my friends, to whom I would like to speak, that it might be injurious to me." Resting that day, he arose on Monday, packed his bags and boarded an afternoon train for North Carolina.

When Lee left Virginia, he was invariably sad. The state was "her," not "it," to him. Years before, when he reached the Old Dominion, he had admitted to his young wife he had "called every flower by name." Lee had only to cross an imaginary state border to feel in exile. For a man of his scope and ability, it is one of the most difficult things in his make-up to explain. In the final analysis, you can't explain it. You have to live in Virginia yourself.

The train now puffed into North Carolina, the state whose rebels had been "first at Bethel, farthest at Gettysburg, and last at Appomattox." With only a ninth of the South's population, North Carolina had furnished a fifth of all the soldiers who fought, and a fourth of all that died in action. In that dying, the South learned a bitter but important lesson. It is possible to believe in a cause strongly, fight for it heroically—and lose.

The days of heroism were definitely past; valor had given way to venality. The very methods and conditions of warfare had obliterated the ideas for which it had been waged. There is as little chance of discovering high idealism in postwar generations as there is of finding a high sense of tragedy in an undertaker. Facing death is one thing. Disposing of corpses is another.

In North Carolina, the state debt had soared in a few years from sixteen to forty million dollars. President Andrew Johnson, himself a native of Raleigh had appointed William Holden provisional governor. Pandora's box was open. By repudiating all past state debt, the 1865 Convention wrought havoc with colleges, banks, and all who held state bonds. When an angry citizenry voted to make Jonathan Worth, rather than Holden, governor, Northerners took this as a sign of continuing disloyalty. Organizing carpetbaggers and Negroes, the Republicans reinstated Holden. The 1868 state convention saw one hundred and seven Republicans run roughshod over the thirteen Democrats, and prompted this sarcastic headline in the Raleigh *Sentinel:*

THE CONSTITUTIONAL CONVENTION (SO-CALLED)—
CORN FIELD AND ETHIOPIAN MINSTRELSY!

Corruption was most blatant in education and railroads. In the year of Lee's visit, state schools received only $38,000 of the $136,000 allotted to them. George Swepson, president of the Western North Carolina Railroad, paid "General" Milton Littlefield $240,000 to influence the legislature.

Unable to check abuses and corruption by legal methods, the conservatives resorted to extra-legal ones. Springing up in 1867, the Ku Klux Klan fought back with secret meetings, mystic signs, intimidation, whippings and lynchings. The Radical Republicans decided to take stern measures. Four months before Lee arrived, the legislature passed the Schoffner Act, empowering the government to place any part of the state under martial law. A few weeks after Lee's visit, Governor Holden invoked this power. He put several counties under Colonel George Kirk, the notoriously unpopular commander of a Carolina regiment that had fought in the Union Army. The situation was explosive. Newspapers carried notices like this one in the Raleigh *Sentinel:* "Governor Holden, you white-livered miscreant! You villain, come and arrest a man, and order your secret clubs not to molest women and children. Yours with contempt and defiance, Josiah Turner, Jr."

Later on Holden would be impeached for "high crimes and misdemeanors," found guilty and removed from office.

Staunch Republican H. R. Helper admitted: "One of the greatest evils affecting society in North Carolina is the incompetent and worthless state and federal officials now in power. They are for the most part pestiferous ulcers feeding upon the body politic."

Lee would not engage in any local social and political wrangling. His thoughts centered on another world—that to which his daughter Annie had gone. Having spent Monday night with the Whites in Warrenton Spring, the Lees arose at dawn to visit the cemetery. In their wagon they carried masses of white hyacinths and gray moss to twine around the base of the monument. Thanking those who had helped Annie while she was alive, the General described the morning as "mournful, yet soothing to my feelings." After he left the grave, his mind continued to center on nature. "The woods are filled with flowers," he observed, "yellow jasmine covers all the trees, and fresh vegetables everywhere." No day of the trip seemed to satisfy him more.

Now the time had come to put aside private tears and accept public acclaim. Men, women, children; planters, servants, tenants; Confederates, carpetbaggers, scalawags; the robust, ailing, maimed—assembled and shouted and cried and stood in awed silence. "Why should they care to see me?" Lee would ask, as crowds gathered and clamored for him. "I am only a poor old Confederate." This very reticence and humility only attracted people all the more.

"Namesakes appeared on the way, of all sizes," Agnes wrote, "the sweetest little children, dressed to their eyes, with bouquets of japonica, or tiny cards in their little fat hands, with their names . . . Old ladies stretched their heads into the windows at way-stations, and then drew back and said, 'He is mighty like his pictures.' "

Lee was "locked up and mum" when the train pulled into Raleigh, North Carolina. Still the huge crowd would not disperse. Whenever he wouldn't come out, food and gifts were put on the train for him. "Even soldiers on the train sent in fruit," wrote Agnes, "and I think we were expected to die of eating."

Over the newly repaired tracks they rolled, westward to Salisbury, then south to Charlotte. There the ovation was overwhelming. By now, word had been flashed ahead by railroad telegraphers. The General, moving south on the Charlotte, Columbia, and Augusta Railroad, would soon be in South Carolina. On they rolled over the clicking track, into the deeply wounded and largely unreconstructed Deep South. Lee watched the landscape change, smelled the sweet spring flowers, saw the woodlands rich in magnolia trees and red buds, gazed at the gray moss hanging like beards on bedraggled Confederate generals.

If the physical situation was lovely, the human landscape was not. Sidney Andrews, an earlier visitor, had found in South Carolina "enough woe and want and ruin and ravage to satisfy the most insatiate heart." The song told about General Sherman "Marching through Georgia." Actually Sherman had done more damage in South Carolina, pillaging a path across the state forty miles wide. The New York *Herald* correspondent who followed the whole campaign wrote: "As for wholesale burnings, pillage, and devastation committed in South Carolina, magnify all I have said of Georgia some fifty-fold, and then throw in an occasional murder, 'jis to bring an old hard-fisted cuss to his senses,' and you have a good idea of the whole thing."

Famous for its gracious homes and gardens, the capital at Columbia had been gutted and burned. Eighty-four of the one hundred and twenty-four blocks had been reduced to ashes. Charred chimneys remained to give ghostly hints of past glories.

A quarter of South Carolina's arms-bearing population and half of all property values, were lost in the War. Many who came back were in plights not unlike that of General Butler, who had "one leg, a wife and three children to support, 70 emancipated slaves, $15,000 debt, and $1.75 in cash." The poet, William Gilmore Simms, going to bed hungry every night, took for himself the nickname "Prince of the Dolefuls." Haughty ladies were reduced to the wash tub and cook pot. Those gentlemen whose luck held out were able to cheat starvation by taking government rations.

Corruption still permeated statehouse, courthouse, courtroom and city hall. Dixie had been subject to such immorality and private plundering that government seemed transformed into an engine of destruction. The Radicals were chanting little ditties like this one, highlighting the infamous career of General Ben "Beast" Butler:

> High diddle diddle
> The Radical fiddle,
> The War closed a little too soon.
> The little dogs laugh
> When Butler and staff
> Ran away with another teaspoon.

The antics of the South Carolina legislature scandalized the nation. Having installed two hundred six richly embossed cuspidors, the carpetbaggers and Negroes stripped the cupboard clean. "They took everything they desired," noted the Senate clerk, Josephus Woodruff, "from swaddling cloth and cradle to the coffin of the undertaker." The "Rule of the Robbers" had begun and it would last long after General Lee had come and gone. Lack of ability, as well as lack of morality, brought on the sorry mess. In South Carolina's 1868 Convention, seventy-six of the delegates were newly emancipated Negroes, of whom only seventeen were taxpayers. Their governor, Ohio-born R. K. Scott, was induced to sign one of the more notorious pieces of legislation while he was intoxicated. As aristocratic Robert Goodwyn Rhett said: "Every appropriation carries enough to pay for the passage of the bill authorizing it."

Knowing some of these things, Lee must have been sick at heart as he pulled into decimated Columbia. Rain was pouring down. Confederate veterans, used to rainy musters, defied the weather and marched smartly to the railroad station. Alexander Haskell, who had commanded the Seventh South Carolina Cavalry, was there; so was General Porter Alexander who had conducted the Gettysburg bombardment preceding Pickett's charge. After the usual acclaim and bravado, the train continued its journey westward through Lexington and Aiken counties toward the Georgia border.

Seldom had Lee been so lonely. Surrounded, often overwhelmed by admirers, he continued to doubt the meaning of their demonstrations and his own ability to withstand many more. Agnes was worried about him, as her letters plainly show. There was, however, no turning back now. Somehow —Lee must hold up to the end.

Late Wednesday night they reached Augusta where the old lion was expected to roar once again. Too tired to move on that day, Lee decided to stay over until Thursday. We know something of the crowd and its surging from the account of a small boy who had to fight and claw his way forward to see the Great Man. Years later, this lad would himself learn the dangers of idolatry. His name was Woodrow Wilson.

More screams and serenades; then the General's train was rolling across Georgia again, southeastward along the Savannah River toward the coast. It was a depressing stage of a trying journey. Besides all her man-inflicted woes, Georgia had suffered almost total crop failures in 1865 and 1866. Natives had tried to survive on roots and berries; the weak had starved to death.

The stately rice plantations had disappeared, along with the larger cotton plantations. The problem was not how to plant new crops, but how to survive at all. The average income for farm labor, which had sunk to one hundred twenty-five dollars in 1867, swooped down to eighty-three dollars in 1868. Lee had seen no such poverty in Virginia. Where was the glitter and glory of battle now? Was it for this that he had ordered his men forward, month after month?

If Lee was dazed by what he saw, other visitors were appalled. One of these, J. T. Trowbridge, awarded the palm to the Georgians as "the meanest and most despicable class of people it has ever been my misfortune to meet." When the economy collapses, so does morality. Arson, burglary and horse stealing reached such proportions that the Georgia legislature voted to impose the death penalty for these crimes. Floods of convicts overflowed the penitentiaries. A general lethargy and indifference to education, literature and things of the spirit spread over the neglected land. Labor was demoralized; cash and credit were unavailable. One thing, at least, was left to those who crowded to the stations whenever the train stopped: their respect for Robert E. Lee. What a burden it must have been for him to have realized it!

That he could see this, understand it, and yet not be puffed up by pride, is one of the remarkable and admirable features of Robert E. Lee.

His train reached Savannah in the late afternoon. The largest crowd that had ever gathered there was on hand, filling the train shed and spilling out into the streets. Only a half hour of persistent pushing enabled Lee's hosts to take him the short distance from the train to the waiting carriage. Thousands who saw him at a distance long remembered his noble face and bearing. The perceptive Savannah *Republican* reporter, getting a close look, noted the inexpressible sadness visible in his face. The group went first to General Lawton's house, but Lee was soon taken on from there to Andrew Lowe's where he might sleep more quietly.

It was a wise move. Shortly after his departure, the Comet Band and the Saxe Horse Band arrived at the Lawtons' to play alternately and loudly. General Lawton thanked them in the name of General Lee, who, he said, had already retired. Lest they follow him there, Lawton did not explain that the great man had retired at another house.

Having been stationed in Savannah before the Civil War and having many old friends there, Lee had hoped for quiet walks and conversations. This was not to be. The young United States Army officer who had visited Savannah early in his career was no more. The man who came there now was the hero of the people. The people must see and pursue him. "I do not think traveling in this way procures me much quiet and repose," Lee wrote on April 7, exhibiting his lifelong habit of understatement. He did not seek fame, and he did not reject it. He just lived with it. That proved to be the hardest task of all.

One of Savannah's illustrious citizens was General Joseph E. Johnston, whom Lee had not seen since the war. The two, sitting at opposite ends of a small table, were persuaded to pose for a Savannah photographer. The print is a memorable one. There they are, proud yet pathetic, aged eagles whose eyes and beaks had grown dull in service to a country that was never to be.

Agnes' illness prolonged the stay in Savannah. "She took cold on the journey or on her first arrival, and has been quite sick, but is better now," Lee wrote his wife on April 11. "I perceive no change in the stricture in my chest. If I attempt to walk beyond a very slow gait, the pain is always there." So was the obligation to visit his father's grave. The next day Lee pushed on.

With Agnes and Andrew Lowe, he boarded the steamer, *Nick King*, which sailed between Savannah and Palatka, Florida. Docking at New Brunswick, they were joined by William Nightingale who owned Dungeness, the estate where "Light-Horse Harry" Lee was buried. Then the boat called at Cumberland Island and the party went ashore to the cemetery.

"Agnes decorated my father's grave with beautiful fresh flowers," the General wrote. "I presume it is the last time I shall be able to pay to it my tribute of respect. The cemetery is unharmed and the grave is in good order, though the house at Dungeness has been burned and the island devastated ... Agnes is still weak and seems to suffer constantly from the neuralgia. I still have the pain in my chest whenever I walk."

On the boat sailed, bound for the southernmost Confederate state, Florida. When they reached Jacksonville, so many people rushed aboard that the little ship almost capsized. To save the situation, Lee walked out on deck; a sudden silence fell over the crowd. It spoke a deeper feeling than the loudest huzzahs. A Southerner of that period would as soon have thought of applauding God.

Now they sailed south along the exotic St. John's for Palatka. Gazing at the gaudy, tangled jungle, one could not have guessed how vital the state had been during the Civil War. The third state to join the Confederacy, Florida furnished 15,000 rebel soldiers—a greater number than the state's entire voting population. She was also a major source of Southern food and supplies. While the coastal towns fell early in the war, the interior was defended vigorously. Captain J. J. Dickinson and his men fired so effectively on the Yankee ship *Columbine* that she foundered and surrendered—perhaps the only time in naval history that a warship was captured by cavalry. For this and other feats, Dickinson was dubbed "Knight of the Silver Spurs."

Such heroic acts won fame, but the Confederacy could not win the war. On May 10, 1865, more than a month after Appomattox, Federal troops finally entered Tallahassee and claimed the state. Not all Florida's rebels were there to see it. Many were buried in shallow graves all the way from the Gulf of Mexico to central Pennsylvania. One of them, war-time Governor John Milton, had taken his own life a few days before Lee surrendered his army.

To this same St. John's River, the Confederate Secretary of War Breckinridge had fled in 1865, aided by a four-oared cutter salvaged from the *Columbine*. "The river abounds in cranes, pelicans, and a great number of crocodiles," Breckinridge wrote. From there, he went overland by ox team and sailed safely to Cuba.

In the five ensuing years the usual stock figures had turned up in Reconstruction Florida: the power-hungry carpetbagger, the scheming promoter, the duped Negro, the influence peddler. State printing charges for 1869 exceeded the whole state budget for 1860. Yet not all items were expensive. The legislature disposed of a million acres of public land at a nickel an acre.

The *Nick King* tied up at Orange Mills so Lee could spend the night with the former chief commissary of the Army of Northern Virginia, Colonel Robert G. Cole. On a warm and winsome day the old comrades strolled around the countryside. Lee is reputed to have eaten, for the only time in his life, a yellow-colored citrus fruit several times the size of an orange. It had no commercial value, Cole explained—he just raised a few to amuse his friends. Since they grew in clusters, he called them "grapefruits."

The climate, fruit and fish all delighted Lee. These were among his best days, and they passed quickly. On April 14th, he was back in Jacksonville, surrounded by the people who had unwittingly come to plague his last months on earth. The Lees were shown the recently opened St. James Hotel, which citizens called "the Fifth Avenue Hotel of Florida." If Lee was impressed, he did not say so. After seeing the other sights and spending a night with Colonel Sanderson, the hero and his daughter took the boat back to Savannah.

"Savannah has become very pleasant in the last few days," he wrote as blossoms lined the streets and fields. After a busy week, he boarded the train for Charleston, South Carolina, hoping to make the trip unnoticed. Word leaked out, however, and the usual delegation was on hand. The Bennet home at which he stayed suddenly became the city's focal point. Delegations, military groups, bands and fire units came there. Lee asked C. G. Memminger, the former Confederate Secretary of the Treasury, to respond for him, but the frenzied crowd would accept no substitute. Finally Lee spoke briefly, attributing his reluctance to his indisposition. It was the only "public address" on the whole trip.

Lee was entranced with Charleston. Along cobbled streets Negroes in gaudy cotton bandanas sold molasses candy, ground nut cakes and sassafras beer, protecting their wares with palmetto fly-brushes. The spires of St. Michael's and St. Philip's poked graceful holes in the blue sky and the columns of the South Carolina Society Hall stood like obedient classical soldiers guarding the double-entrance stairways. The sound of laughter crept out of half-hidden courtyards. Old fashioned seemliness prevailed.

Yet just underneath Charleston's picturesque exterior dwelt deep and sullen resentment. "Never, sir," Stephen Powers had thundered, "will any high-toned Southron consent to remain any longer than brute force compels him in a Union controlled by the nutmeg-eyed, muslin-faced Yankee." "Why, oh why, my Southern nigger worshippers," Thomas Woodward had sneered, "will you grope your way through this worse than Egyptian darkness? Why not cease this crawling on your bellies and assume the upright form of men?" To many people of this breed, Lee's policy of peace and reconciliation was an abomination.

There was scant leisure to saunter about, and none to engage in political controversy. The Charleston *Courier* told how Lee's time was spent: "Stately dames of the old school, grandmothers of seventy, and a long train of granddaughters, all flock around the noble old chief." Then came their husbands, sons, in-laws, grandsons, and guests.

Seeking the quiet he seldom achieved, the General started out with Agnes for Wilmington, North Carolina, on April 28th. Again his effort to keep the movement a secret failed. A special train came out to meet him. As Lee transferred from the regular locomotive, the uniformed boys from the Cape Fear Academy presented arms smartly. The gesture drew no comment from one who had seen many young lads salute smartly, then march off into bloody battle. Later that day, Lee requested that there be no more special demonstrations.

Cheered in Wilmington and Weldon, he finally reached the Old Dominion again. At Portsmouth he could board the ferry for Norfolk. He was almost home.

There was, however, more pageantry to come. The Virginians were numerous and tumultuous. Roaring cannon announced his arrival in Portsmouth. Roman candles and rockets heralded his ferry crossing, and more cannon boomed from the Norfolk side. Visibly shaken, Lee reached his nadir in Norfolk. If he had not sought quiet when he did, he might well have died on the road.

If such occasions hurt Lee, his own behavior brought good comment from the nation's press. On May 4, his last day in Norfolk, the Richmond *Inquirer* carried this quotation from the New York *Herald:* "It is pleasant to witness the dignified and temperate course of General Lee in the midst of these heart-felt ovations. The name of Lee is identified with the most heroic deeds of the war for independence, and it is pleasant to find it connected with words and acts of fraternal reconciliation and pacification."

On May 5, the Lees went aboard the steamer that served

the James River plantations. Brandon, Shirley, Carter's Grove, the White House, White Marsh—all these names were synonymous with family, cordiality and quiet. His expectations were fulfilled. "Brandon is very beautiful," he wrote, "and it is refreshing to look at the river." On May 10, he arrived at Shirley where Mrs. Lee had lived as a girl. One of the daughters of the family could not believe that the hero enjoyed having his hands tickled: "We had heard of God, but here was General Lee!" she wrote.

Twenty-five miles north of Shirley, lived Rooney Lee at White House. The General rested here and played with his small grandson and namesake. Moving fifteen miles east, he was a guest of his bachelor son Robert at Romancoke. "He walked and drove over the farm," Robert wrote, "discussed my plans for improvement, and was much interested in all my work, advising me about the site of my new house, new barns, ice house, etc."

At White Marsh, one of the family favorites, "Cousin Rebecca," greeted the General. So fatigued was he now that she begged him to lie down and rest. Lee declined, but he did take a glass of wine. When, at dinner, a young cousin asked what might be in store for "us poor Virginians," the General gave one of his most famous replies: "You can work for Virginia, to build her up again, to make her great again. You can teach your children to love and cherish her."

Leaving the plantation country was painful; he knew instinctively that he would never return. This was more like "home" than Lexington, tucked in its Scotch-Irish valley, Spartan and provincial. In Tidewater Virginia, the Lees had made their name and their history: now the greatest Lee of them all must finish out his self-imposed exile in a distant portion of the Commonwealth few of his illustrious ancestors had ever seen. Still he did not whimper and he did not look back.

There was a four-day stopover in Richmond for shopping, business and leave-taking. A young sculptor, E. V. Valentine, came to measure Lee for a statue.

"I will have to do the modeling in Lexington," he explained.

"You had best make the visit at once," Lee answered.

On May 26, 1870, Robert E. Lee slipped out of the city he had defended for years. He took the train to Charlottesville, then Lynchburg, and finally the packet boat to Lexington. On the morning of May 28, he was home.

He had seen the South at a time when she was struggling to restore some semblance of her life and social structure. The effects of the war were deeper and sharper than he could have imagined: he had seen the bleeding South. But he had also seen courage and fortitude and a new generation coming into power. What impressed him most was the elasticity of her people. "I am astonished," he told a reporter in South Carolina, "to see Charleston so wondrously recuperated after all her disasters."

The patriarch of a great American family, he had paid his final respects to his daughter and father. He had also acted out the role which history had thrust upon him, for thousands of Southerners to see and remember. The surging crowds, more deadly in some ways than advancing armies, had been met and placated. The old soldier had performed a difficult assignment without flinching.

Now it was over. He had come back home to die.

XIV

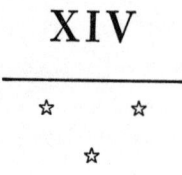

THE VESTRY MEETING

> I was glad when they said unto me, We will go into the house of the Lord.
> —Psalm 122

NOT APRIL BUT SEPTEMBER is Lexington's cruelest month. Blueness gives way to grayness, sunshine to rain. Suddenly, summer is over. A note of death is struck. The maple flames, but quickly dies down. The corn, which was proud and high in the August sun, sags along umber fields. The woods stand brown and lifeless and the trees are bare, ruined choirs.

September 28, 1870, was a day that invited dark thoughts. Students and faculty moved about in a bone-chilling rain and said the wind was too raw for late September. General Lee said his morning prayers and read from the Book of Common Prayer the Psalter appointed for the day: "Praise the Lord, ye house of Israel: praise the Lord, ye house of Aaron. Praise the Lord, ye house of Levi: ye that hear the

Lord, praise the Lord. . . ." Then he went to the morning chapel service. After chapel, his office being in the basement, he did not have to confront the raw wet morning. But he did have to face students adjusting their new fall schedules. This took several hours. He also wrote a letter to Samuel Tagart in Baltimore, in which he struck an optimistic note: "My pains are less and my strength greater. In fact, I suppose I am as well as I shall be. I am still following Dr. B.'s directions, and in time I may improve still more."

As Lee walked out of his office at the morning's end, a sophomore named Percy Davidson asked him to autograph a small picture when it was convenient. "I will go right back and do it now," he said. The visibly tired President then left the chapel, pulling his office shut behind him.

Up the hill he trudged for lunch. Glancing at him, his wife suggested that he spend the rest of the day at home. But there was an important vestry meeting scheduled for four o'clock that afternoon. The General thought he must go. A few minutes before the hour, he pulled an old military cloak over his shoulders, told Mrs. Lee goodbye, and started down the hill to Grace Episcopal Church.

In the damp unheated building, where other vestrymen had already gathered, Lee engaged in a little light conversation with his friends. He told several stories about his old mentor, Bishop William Meade. Lee's physician, Dr. Barton, was there too: later on he would comment that Lee had seemed tired, and that despite the chill of the place, his face was flushed. Glancing at his watch, the General, who was the soul of punctuality, called the meeting to order promptly at four. The Registrar made the customary entry in the Record Book with his florid nineteenth century handwriting:

> *Sept. 28.* At a meeting of the Vestry of the Church, present Gen. R. E. Lee, Gen. F. H. Smith, Prof. Joynes, Col. Johnston, Dr. Barton, Messrs. Figgatt, Koones, Campbell, Dr. Madison and Col. Williamson. Gen. Lee was in the chair.

In a very real sense, Lee was in his spiritual home. The one intimate friend he had in all his life was God.

Not that he was a brilliant theologian, preacher, or prophet. In his religion, as in all aspects of his life, Lee was both child and captive of his cultural heritage. He exemplifies the stereotyped, low-church Episcopalianism followed by most upper-class Virginians of his day. He accepted rather than challenged the phrases and dogmas which were his heritage at baptism and confirmation. The stormy battle between science and religion, which gripped his contemporaries, did not affect him. The pious predictable phrases which came to Lee's lips were no mask. They were truly representative of the man.

Everywhere and always God was in his heart. Most of his private letters and military dispatches expressed trust and confidence in God. Lee never tired of acknowledging his dependence on Divine Providence. His piety was apparently inexhaustible. It is a chief motif of his life after Appomattox.

Centuries of religious and ecclesiastical devotion shaped those countless invocations by the Chief of the Army of Northern Virginia. In medieval England, a paternal ancestor, Lionel Lee, marched with Richard the Lion-Hearted on the Third Crusade and was rewarded by being made the first Earl of Litchfield. Not one but two Lee banners hung in Saint George's Chapel, Windsor. During the Reformation the Lees were staunch Anglicans. Richard Lee, founding father of the American branch, was notably pious and bequeathed his soul "to me blessed Redeemer, Jesus Christ." For generations the Lees were intimately linked with Virginia's established Anglican church which directed the colony's spiritual and sacramental life.

During Robert E. Lee's childhood, his family communed at Christ Church, Alexandria, where George Washington himself had been a pew holder. The young pastor who taught the Lee children the catechism, William Meade, later became one of Virginia's most beloved Episcopal bishops. As a result of his early training, Lee boasted that he could recite the catechism before he could read.

His mother, a deeply religious woman, implanted within him an ineradicable belief in prayer and God's interposition in everyday affairs. Later on, Robert did not have to place God in the center of his thinking; he just left Him where He naturally was. His wife's family, the Carters, were as Episcopal as the Lees. Robert Carter, Mrs. Lee's great-great-grandfather, built and endowed Christ Church in Lancaster County at his own expense. "King" Carter, an imperious planter, did not hesitate to order his curate to pray for rain. Naturally, the wedding of Robert E. Lee and his bride Mary was conducted according to the service in the Book of Common Prayer. The Reverend Dr. Ruel Keith, of the Episcopal Theological Seminary near Alexandria, officiated. Six years later, starting west with his army unit, Lee wrote home to Mary in her stately mansion, Arlington: "I pray God to watch over and direct our efforts in guarding our dear little son that we may bring him up in the way he should go." The sentence and the sentiment were typical. Custis, and the six children that followed him, were all baptized at Arlington by the Reverend Charles B. Dana.

Stationed at Fort Hamilton in New York Harbor in 1843, Lee was promptly elected to the Episcopal vestry there. The Tractarian Movement, then raging throughout the Anglican church, made itself felt in this small congregation, and "Low Church" members suspected the rector of "High Church" views. Lee would not get mixed up in such arguments, then or later on. To him, they had nothing to do with the essential truth of Christianity. He worshipped God, not the church. On Easter day, 1857, he wrote home from the West: "My services have been performed alone in my tent, I hope with a humble, grateful, and penitent heart, and will be acceptable to our Heavenly Father."

Shortly afterward, when a small boy died in camp, Lee obliged the family by conducting the funeral. "For the first time in my life I read the beautiful funeral service of our Episcopal church over the grave," he wrote. Another child died soon afterward, and he was once more asked to conduct the service. "I hope I shall not be called on again, for it wrings a parent's heart with anguish that is painful to see," he confided to Mrs. Lee. The officer who stood beside those two small wooden caskets being lowered into the vast Texas plains had not faced death often in his military career. In the decade ahead, however, he would stare—not at one—but at hundreds of young corpses, boys who had died carrying out his orders. A crescendo of anguish such as America had never heard would rise. The Lee who hoped he would not be called upon again would be summoned—many times.

The Civil War and Reconstruction tested the mettle of men, creeds and religions. The daily presence of death taught Americans profound truths about life. Crises are crucibles in which human beings are subjected to human and inhuman stress and strain; tests of their integrity and immortality. Under such circumstances, politicians like Jefferson Davis and generals like Burnside were tried and found wanting. Leaders like Lincoln and generals like Lee emerged from the searing fire, not destroyed but refined.

In the major decision of his life—whether to preserve the larger Union or to fight for the smaller unit within it—Lee made what some have considered the wrong decision. At a time when nationalism was working its evil spell, Lee worshipped a lesser idol: statism. Yet he tried to relate his decision to no earthly state, but to Providence. Eventually all his acts were set in a theological framework. Believing that slavery and secession were evil, he entered the war with a sense of guilt. "May He in His great mercy shield us from the calamity our sins have produced." He prayed, further, that he himself be enabled to perform his duty and not be tempted beyond his strength. It was remarkably like the prayer of another great American on the other side of the Potomac: Abraham Lincoln.

Despite his Cavalier background and manner, Lee could on occasion be as stern as his Presbyterian lieutenant, Stonewall Jackson. In the dreary days of defeat and the demanding days of Reconstruction, a vein of iron came to the surface of Lee's character. He strongly condemned drinking, gambling, and profanity; attributed Confederate failures to Confederate sins; and approved of fast days and prayer meetings. His general orders about the Sabbath had a Cromwellian ring:

> The Commanding General directs that none but duties strictly necessary shall be required to be performed on

Sunday and that all labor, both of men and animals, which it is practicable to anticipate or postpone, or the immediate performance of which is not essential to the safety, health, or comfort of the army, shall be suspended on that day.

Lee learned to bottle up his own emotions and to display an incredible self-control in that most demanding of human roles—playing God to the thousands of human beings serving under him. No more poignant example of his self-control exists than that he showed at the news of the death of his daughter Annie in 1863. Lee's aide, Colonel Walter Taylor, relates the episode in *Four Years with General Lee*. Lee received and read his mail, after which Taylor appeared with a list of routine matters. Lee reviewed them carefully and gave his orders. "I left him, but for some cause returned in a few moments, and with accustomed freedom entered his tent without announcement," Taylor writes. "I was startled and shocked to see him overcome with grief, an open letter on his knees. That letter contained the news of his daughter's death . . . His army demanded his first thought and care: to his men and their needs he must first attend. Only then could he surrender to his private, personal affliction."

Even so, no one can say that Lee was cold or unemotional. Concerning Annie's death, he wrote to another daughter, Mary Custis: "In the quiet hours of the night when there is nothing to lighten the full weight of my grief, I feel as if I should be overwhelmed. I have always counted, if God should spare me a few days after this Civil War was ended, that I should have Annie with me, but year after year my hopes go out, and I must be resigned." And to his own wife, Lee confided: "I cannot express the anguish I feel at the death of our sweet Annie. To know that I shall never see her again on earth, that her place in our circle, which I always hoped one day to enjoy, is forever vacant, is agonizing in the extreme ... I wish I could give you comfort, but beyond our hope in the great mercy of God, and the belief that He takes her at the time and place when it is best for her to go, there is none. May the same mercy be extended to us all, and may we be prepared for His summons."

If only his closest associates saw how Lee's heart was wrung and his faith tested by Annie's death, many knew that he reached the valley of despair as Stonewall Jackson lay dying after he had been shot accidentally by his own men at Chancellorsville. To Jackson's chaplain, the Reverend B. T. Lacy, Lee cried out: "Oh sir, he must not die! Surely God will not visit us with such a calamity. If I have ever prayed in my life, I have pleaded with the Lord that Jackson might be spared to us."

Jackson was not spared. Yet when he died, Lee was able quickly to humble himself before the Deity he had all but challenged. "God's will be done," he wrote. "I trust He will raise someone in his place." Who was there to raise up? For mighty Stonewall, there was no equal.

Yet Lee fought on, to the crest at Gettysburg, where he was turned back by circumstances and decisions which have not become clearer after a century's debate. As we have already seen, Lee blamed no one but himself for the defeat and offered his resignation to President Davis. It was, of course, refused. Endorsing a day of fasting and prayer in August, 1863, Lee issued a proclamation beginning: "Soldiers! We have sinned against Almighty God. We have forgotten his signal mercies and have cultivated a revengeful, haughty, and boastful spirit. Let us humble ourselves before Him. Let us confess our many sins and beseech Him to give us a higher courage, a purer patriotism, and a more determined will."

As the Confederacy's military might declined, the soldiers' religious zeal increased. In 1863, a revival swept through the ranks. Prayer meetings flourished. Lee frequently took part in these and never failed to listen to exhortations from one of his ragged Rebels. In both private and public worship the General was so ardent that his chaplains believed he was more concerned with winning souls than battles. Perhaps they were right.

Consider this episode, for example, in November, 1863. Facing Meade at Mine Run, Lee rushed down the line of battle with his general staff as the enemy artillery belched forth its dull thunder. Seeing a group of tattered veterans bowed in prayer, he instantly dismounted, uncovered his head and joined devoutly in the worship.

Fortunately, Lee's religious fervor was matched by religious tolerance. He de-emphasized denominational preferences. A routine application by a Jewish soldier for permission to attend services in Richmond's synagogue came to him with this notation by the man's regimental captain: "Disapproved. If such applications were granted, the whole army would turn Jews or Shaking Quakers."

Lee reversed the decision and wrote: "Approved, and respectfully returned to Captain _____, with the advice that he should always respect the religious views and feelings of others."

Lee seldom spoke harshly of the enemy. He fought the North because it invaded his homeland, seeking to wrest from the South certain sacred rights. "I have never cherished bitter or vindictive feelings," he said, "and have never seen the day when I did not pray for the enemy." This must have become increasingly difficult as the Union's success increased and the South failed more and more. Lee did not blame this on Providence, but on himself. "You see what a poor sinner I am, and how unworthy to possess what was given me," he wrote. "For that reason it has been taken away."

As Grant's shells crashed into Petersburg, Lee regularly attended Sunday services of the local Episcopal minister. To another clergyman, the Reverend Mr. Cole, he wrote, "We must suffer patiently to the end, when all things will be made right."

After General E. P. Alexander recommended that the troops disperse for guerrilla warfare, Lee replied: "General, you and I as Christian men have no right to consider only how this would affect us. We would bring on a state of affairs it would take the country years to recover from." For Lee, the Christian principles that made war unavoidable also made surrender inevitable. He related this, like all his decisions, to a larger pattern than that of his own life.

Thus, in 1865 he came to Lexington more as a missionary than an educator. He did not speak often of "Christian education" because it never occurred to him that any other kind was worth considering. Yet he took care to affiliate with a college that was not controlled by any denomination or sect. To him, religion was a freedom to be enjoyed, not a law to be enforced. In this he was profoundly Protestant. "I find it so hard to keep one poor sinner's heart in the right way," he told his friends, "that it seems presumptuous to try to keep others."

Although the Anglican church had come to the Valley before the Revolution, it had never flourished in that Presbyterian stronghold. Grace Episcopal Church was not built in Lexington until 1844, and had only a few dozen active members before the Civil War. Lee had hardly arrived in town before he was elected to the vestry on September 26, 1865. He made known at once his Christian sentiments. To the trustees of Washington College, the President-elect said: "I dread the thought of any student going from the college without becoming a sincere Christian." These sentiments he repeated time and again during his presidency. Lee's intellectual and spiritual missions were too organically blended to be separated.

The financial situation of the little Episcopal congregation, struggling to maintain a rector and parsonage and to contribute to a nearby mission, was precarious. A proposal was made "to sell the parsonage, with a view of extinguishing the debt on same, and provide one within our means." This, however, was not done. Instead on, April 13, 1867, the vestry assigned pew rents, starting at forty dollars for the first eight rows in the center, and going down to twenty dollars for the back pews. The Lees rented one of the forty dollar pews, four from the front and directly behind ex-Governor Letcher, but the realistic vestry realized that many pews would remain unoccupied, and so it was "proper to reserve some as free pews." Later on, to avoid embarrassment, they authorized the rector and warden to assign pews to persons unable to pay the assessment.

If the church were economically shaky, it was doctrinally sound. At the beginning of each year, Lee joined with his fellow vestrymen to sign a statement which read: "I do yield my hearty assent and approbation to the doctrines and worship of the Protestant Episcopal Church in the United States, and promise that I will faithfully execute the office of a Vestryman of Latimer Parish in Rockbridge County without prejudice, favor, or affection, according to the best of my skill and knowledge."

A devoted vestryman and communicant, Lee spent more time wrestling with the church's financial problems than with any other during his Lexington years. As involved as he was with his official college duties, Lee also served intermittently as the chairman of Grace Church's Finance Committee. In an 1868 report signed by him, he pointed out that the church was in arrears to the pastor for forty dollars and twenty-one cents of his 1867 salary and one hundred and ninety-one dollars of his 1868 salary. The committee recommended that parishioners be urged to pay their arrears as soon as possible, and also "begged leave to state, that in their opinion $800 is an insufficient salary for the decent support of the Pastor." Lee was not only instrumental in having the stipend raised. He personally made up the salary deficit in the 1870 budget.

Lee's concern with proselyting his students became almost an obsession. Speaking of this subject, Dr. J. William Jones reported, Lee's eyes overflowed with tears and his lips quivered as he exclaimed: "Oh, Doctor, if I could only know that all the young men in the College were good Christians, I should have nothing more to desire." This from a man who did not shed a tear at Gettysburg, Cold Harbor or Appomattox.

The Bible was by all odds Lee's favorite book. He thought it "sufficient to satisfy all human desires," adding: "The difficulty is to conform the heart and mind and thoughts to its teaching, and to obtain strength to bring the body under the control of the spirit."

When English friends sent Lee a Bible, he called it "a

book in comparison with which all others in my eyes are of minor importance, and which in all my perplexities and distresses has never failed to give me light and strength." And even though he resisted countless invitations to join and sponsor groups, he not only joined the Rockbridge Bible Society, but served as its president.

Lee not only rejoiced over religious conversions among students and cadets at the two Lexington colleges, but he publicly praised them. During "the great V.M.I. revival of 1869," over a hundred young men made their professions of faith. "That is the best news I have heard since I have been in Lexington," Lee said. "Would that we could have such a revival in our college, and all our colleges."

An ardent revivalist, Lee was neither liturgist nor legalist. He did not engage in spirited arguments on churchmanship or doctrine. "I never trouble myself about such questions," he replied, when asked about the apostolic succession. "My chief concern is to try to be a humble, sincere Christian myself." A Lexington lady complained that she had trouble finding appropriate food for Lenten fasts. Lee replied: "I would not trouble myself with special dishes. I suppose if we try to abstain from special sins, that is all that will be expected of us."

On several occasions Lee's fellow vestrymen prevailed upon him to represent the parish at out-of-town meetings. In the spring of 1869 he even left the College right before examinations in order to attend a council meeting at Fredericksburg. At this and other meetings of the sort, Lee took no part in the council's debate, though he agreed to serve as a member of committees. Having social obligations in Fredericksburg, Lee happened to be absent when the Council discussed the admission of delegates from a Negro church. However, he was said to be strongly in favor of the decision that they should be seated.

Because he favored sermons and prayers that were short and pertinent, he praised a preacher who gave "the very marrow of the Gospel." Nor did Lee mind suggesting, indirectly, that the young man who helped with chapel services "confine his morning prayers to us poor sinners at the college, and pray for the Turks, the Jews, the Chinese, and the other heathens some other time." His Christianity, like his life, was rooted in reality. He expected no millenium during his sojourn on earth. "Mankind for years will not be sufficiently Christianized to bear the absence of restraint and force," he said. Yet he did not overestimate the role of a soldier. Once, when his daughter Mildred was writing a paper on the farmer, soldier, and sailor, Lee said: "The first is the most useful citizen, the last two necessary evils which will disappear when the world becomes sufficiently Christianized."

Lee's social and religious codes were compatible, not antithetical. He aspired to be a Christian gentleman and did not think the two concepts could be separated. It is hard to dissect Lee's thoughts and actions because he was not a compartmentalized man. His life and personality were organic and unified. Of course, there had to be a central pivot around which he turned. That pivot was not, as many have said, military. It was not social; certainly it was not intellectual. It was religious.

XV

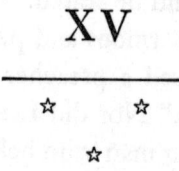

THE VIGIL

*A Prince once said of a Monarch slain,
"Taller he seems in Death."*
—Ancient Folk Tale

ON CLEAR AUTUMN NIGHTS in the valley of Virginia, the stars shine through like ten thousand golden pinpricks in the black glass dome girding the Blue Ridge and the Alleghenies. Chill breezes come down from the north, bending the pliant willows, but not the white oaks holding fast and waiting stoically for the dawn.

On such a night—October 14, 1870—a handful of young men sat silently around a coffin. Inside, dressed in plain black civilian clothes, was a man who had once worn a general's uniform and threatened the life of his nation—Robert E. Lee. These were the honored few who had been allowed to keep a sleepless vigil as he began his unending sleep.

Two days earlier, after a fortnight of illness and suffering, he had died. For two weeks he had not smiled once, though he had greeted his family and friends with the pressure of his hand. To have seen him then would have shocked many who had known and admired him earlier in life. He did not look like the Greek god who had prepared to do battle only a decade earlier, or the blameless victim who had had the grace to accept defeat and to fight on with his influence rather than with his sword. As Stephen Vincent Benét imagined it:

> But there is nothing ruined in his face,
> And nothing beaten in those steady eyes.
> If he's grown old, it isn't like a man,
> It's more the way a river might grow old.

"I do not like his complexion," Mrs. Lee had said when he returned from his Southern trip in April, 1870. "He seems very stiff." His pace was slower, his hair whiter, his eyes dimmer than they had been a year earlier. What his doctors labeled rheumatism was in fact angina pectoris, probably accompanied by arteriosclerosis. Days of unending jabbing pain followed. Now the marble-white face set against the black casket lining showed that all the earthly suffering was over.

He had neither expected nor wanted to recover. For several months he had treated death as inevitable and not altogether undesirable. "I am too old for the work I am trying to do," he had admitted months earlier. When he attended his brother's funeral in Richmond during the summer of 1869, Lee wrote to his wife: "May God bless us all and preserve us for the time when we, too, must part, the one from the other, which is now close at hand."

What he expected he did not fear. If we cannot say he

lacked the will to live once he was struck down, we can at least say he accepted his plight without a murmur or a struggle to reverse what seemed inevitable. In this, his loyal admirers thought, nature concurred. Early in October, as he was sinking, a flashing aurora illumined the heavens above Lexington. His Lexington neighbor, Mrs. McDonald, took her book of Scottish poems off the shelf and showed this quatrain to her neighbors:

> All night long the northern streamers
> Shot across the sky:
> Fearful lights, that never beckon
> Save when kings or heroes die.

Two local physicians, Doctors H. S. Barton and R. L. Madison, attended Lee and did all they could. The attack, they noted, resembled concussion of the brain, without the attendant swoon. Despite impaired consciousness and a tendency to doze, they reported "no paralysis of motion or sensation, and no evidence of suffering or inflammation of the brain." They treated it like a case of what was then called "venous congestion," and were elated when he became strong enough to sit up and take nourishment. He answered questions, usually in monosyllables. But he neither expected nor wanted to get well. When his son Custis spoke cheerfully of his recovery, his father merely shook his head and pointed upward.

"How do you feel today, General?" Dr. Madison asked during the second week of illness.

"I feel better," Lee said, slowly but distinctly.

"You must haste and get well. Traveller has been standing so long in the stable that he needs exercise."

This time the General made no reply. Instead, he shook his head slowly and closed his eyes. Later on that day he said softly, "It is of no use."

On October 10, in the early afternoon, Lee's pulse became rapid, his breathing hurried and his face flushed. He got worse as the day advanced, and by midnight he was seized with severe shivering. No brave promises came to the family's lips now.

The next day he refused both medicine and nourishment. The mind, so carefully disciplined over many years, began to wander, and long-silent cannon began to boom again. Half-coherent orders were given and long-submerged phrases were released. Then came words so clear and emphatic that everyone near him understood them: "Tell Hill he *must* come up!"

Through the night, Mrs. Lee sat close to her husband, holding his hand. He would not recognize her, or anyone else, again. At dawn, October 12, he was barely alive, having held on precariously since his terminal illness started. Shortly after nine o'clock he gave his last order. "Strike the tent," he said. Then he died.

The town was already blanketed in gloom that turned quickly into mourning. Bells rang, stores closed, college classes were dismissed. The doctors prepared an official statement on his death for the newspapers: "mental and physical fatigue, inducing venous congestion of the brain, which, however, never proceeded so far as apoplexy or paralysis, but gradually caused cerebral exhaustion and death."

A few days earlier, flood waters had swept through Lexington, destroying wharves and bridges, cutting the town off from the outside world. Mr. C. M. Koones' shipment of coffins from Richmond had been swept away, so that not one was to be had in the community. Two young men, Charles Chittum and Harry Wallace, began a search. They found a coffin which had washed over the dam and lodged two miles down river on a small island. Because it was a little short, Lee was buried without his shoes.

At nine on the morning of October 14, three ministers delivered eulogies—the Reverend William N. Pendleton, the Reverend W. S. White, and the Reverend J. William Jones. Mr. Pendleton's talk, the main one, was based on the Thirty-Seventh Psalm:

> Commit thy way unto the Lord, and put thy trust in Him, and He shall bring it to pass.
> He shall make thy righteousness as clear as the light, and thy just dealing as the noon-day.
> Hold these still in the Lord, and abide patiently upon Him . . .

At half past one Lee's body was taken from the President's house to the chapel, to rest in state until the next morning. On that night the final vigil was held.

By now not only the college buildings, but all the local hotels, churches and stores were draped in mourning. Flags were at half-mast. On the morning of the fifteenth, the funeral procession made its slow solemn way around the town. All signs of military glory were absent. Confederate veterans wore only black lapel ribbons as distinguishing marks; no flags flew.

The Escort of Honor—former Confederate soldiers—and the clergymen preceded the hearse. Directly behind walked Traveller, the attending physicians, and Washington College's trustees and faculty. Starting at the President's house, the procession moved along Washington and Jefferson Streets to Main Street, where various dignitaries joined, then past the Court House to the Virginia Military Institute. Minute guns were fired from the parapet, and the whole corps of cadets presented arms. Moving up to the College Chapel, overflowing with spectators, the funeral service began.

The Episcopal burial service was conducted by the Reverend William N. Pendleton. No eulogium was given. Then the body was carried to the vault, in the basement of the chapel, which had been prepared for its reception. The committal was read from the bank on the southern side of the chapel, in front of the vault. The body was deposited in its last resting place. The earthly life of Robert E. Lee was over.

XVI

THE GUARDIAN ANGEL

> Angels and ministers of grace defend us!
> —Shakespeare

LEE'S LIFE after Appomattox can be summed up in six words: retreat, resurgence, reconciliation, resignation, death and resurrection.

The growth of the Lee legend after Appomattox, and the uses to which it has been put, provide one of the best barometers of Southern thought and temper in the last century.

The very day of his funeral men anticipated the apotheosis. In Lexington they formed the Memorial Association which soon became a standard fixture in Southern towns. People with no pennies to spare put pennies aside to help buy statues of the Great Man. "What would Lee have done?" became the yardstick by which every conceivable activity and decision could be measured. Orators rifled the dictionary for laudatory adjectives. The tiny Victorian chapel in which the General was buried became, instantly, a shrine.

Some men are what we ourselves would like to be. Their example thrills and inspires us. Their name conjures up both a figure and a feeling. We call them heroes.

All people need and crave heroes, but none so much as those whose other possessions have been destroyed. In 1865 the North had the victory. Social and economic control of the nation was plainly in Yankee hands. But the South had Robert E. Lee. Nothing could alter that.

Up until 1870, the South had Lee in the flesh. After that, they looked to him as to a guardian angel. In the second role he was, if anything, more powerful and pervasive.

I have myself stood at the deathbed of a lovely Southern lady and heard her say: "I'm not afraid to die. I expect to go to heaven. There I'll see three whom I've always loved—my husband, Jesus, and Robert E. Lee."

Given to an heroic interpretation of history, ex-Confederates soon forgot the stench of battle, the wounded screaming for aid, and the dying convulsed in misery. They talked of glorious charges—not of mangled bodies strewn on hillsides, or corpses blackened by frost. The horror of Gettysburg, the hunger of Petersburg, and the anguish of Appomattox faded. What they remembered was the rebel yell, the thin gray line of heroes, and the General mounted on Traveller. Did they really remember Lee or—as James Street says in *The Civil War*—"the archangel Michael, away off yonder beyond reach—pure, white, godly, cold"?

A new post-war generation of Southerners realized that Lee's doctrine of reconciliation, in economic, if not in social realms, was the only course for Dixie. They followed the Pied Piper of Atlanta, Henry Grady, who proclaimed: "We have smoothed the path Southward, wiped out the place where Mason and Dixon's line used to be, and hung out the latchstring to you and yours."

The rancor of the Old South was lost in the smoke and bustle of the New. Ironically, no single reputation benefited so much from this change as that of the Old South's paragon, Robert E. Lee. The ideas he had enunciated after Appomattox exactly fitted the needs of an ambitious, industrial-minded middle class.

Though he had almost wrecked the Union, Lee was soon accepted as a national hero. After Reconstruction and the period of hysteria, the North wanted to get on with the business of becoming a major world power. A united and vigorous nation was the prerequisite. When the South joined enthusiastically in the Spanish-American War—a Lee, Fitzhugh, served as a major general—most Northerners were ready to forget the civil insurrection.

By then, Lee had won Northern acclaim from several impressive quarters. One strong supporter, Charles Francis Adams, was the quintessence of New Englandism. Descended from two Yankee presidents, son of the Union's Civil War Ambassador to England, he had faced Lee at Gettysburg. Now he praised him. By prohibiting guerrilla warfare, Adams argued, Lee saved both sides untold misery. Magnanimous and bold, Lee was a patriot, not a traitor. "Under similar conditions I would myself have done exactly what Lee did," Adams announced. "In fact, I do not see how I, placed as he was placed, could have done otherwise."

Valiant in war, self-contained in victory, superb in defeat, Lee was worthy of the best steel. Adams looked forward to the day when Lee would be placed in the national Pantheon.

"His bronze effigy, mounted on his charger and with the insignia of his Confederate rank, will, from its pedestal in the nation's capital, gaze across the Potomac at his old home at Arlington."

A leading Yankee biographer, Gamaliel Bradford, joined the ranks of Lee's admirers. Eighth in descent from Governor William Bradford of Plymouth Colony, Bradford too had ample Northern credentials. In *Lee, the American* he put Lee's reputation on a national plateau from which it has never descended. "I have loved Lee," Bradford wrote, "and I may say that his influence upon my own life has been as deep and as inspiring as any I have ever known."

A generation later, Lee's life was given its most detailed and exemplary presentation by a Virginian, Douglas Southall Freeman. His four-volume *R. E. Lee* won wide acclaim, as did the three later volumes, *Lee's Lieutenants*. For Southerners, Freeman was *the* scholar of *the* man who led *the* war. Despite claims of impartiality, he was writing a defense as well as a biography. Believing in the tournament theory of war, Freeman meticulously sketched the golden days of the great knights. He was the Virginia gentleman writing eloquently about other Virginia gentlemen.

At the end of his study, Freeman brings us close to Lee's open coffin. "There he lies. Now that they have shrouded him, with his features so white against the lining of the casket that he seems already a marble statue for the veneration of the South. His cause died at Appomattox; now, in him, it is to have its apotheosis."

So it has been. In a few years Lee has become remote as with the flight of centuries. The little town of Lexington has become "The Shrine of the South." Locks of Lee's hair, his eating utensils, crumbled newspaper clippings, and the skeleton of his horse Traveller are reverently displayed in the Lee Chapel Museum. Markers about Lee exploits and movements dot the Southern landscape. Perorations about Lee have continued to be fulsome and—occasionally—even blasphemous.

Speaking in the Virginia Senate in 1940, Henry T. Wickham said: "Some have likened Lee's last word 'Strike the tent' to the last words of the Savior, 'It is finished.' I believe when Lee uttered those words that a vision of glory appeared before his closing eyes. He heard a trumpet sound and lo! a troop cometh, and encompassed by a cloud of witnesses a veteran pilgrim essayeth the flood."

In making clear what Lee is to them, his followers also manifest what qualities they admire in heroes. They put a higher value on integrity and endurance than on brilliance or profundity. What is ultimately pleasing is a well-proportioned life and the beauty of his conduct. Lee did not depend so much upon the search for truth as upon the softening quality of an atmosphere and a strong irreducible core of tradition. Lee knew what he loved: his state, his land, his family, his God. He was a product of a provincial but proud aristocracy, bound together by Anglo-Saxon ideology and the force of a gloriously remembered past.

A devout, literal-minded Christian, Lee practiced a peculiarly Southern form of Shintoism. He knew who were "his sisters and his cousins and his aunts"—and he reckoned them by the dozens. As a family they attended the same Episcopal services which had served as a bond between the state Charles II had called "the Old Dominion" and Mother England. With the Civil War a whole chapter in American history closed. For the South, Lee had closed that chapter—in word and in deed.

Lee baffles those who study him today, much as he did those who fought him in earlier days. His is the mystery of no mystery; the armor without a significant flaw. The whole experience can be exasperating. Wrote Henry Adams, classmate of Robert E. Lee's son Rooney at Harvard: "The habit of command was not enough, and the Virginian had little else. He was simply beyond analysis; so simple that even the simple New England student could not realize him."

Like father, like son. Certainly neither Robert nor Rooney Lee had the intellectual acumen of the Adamses. Still, they were solid; they could make and implement decisions; they were rocks in adversity. They lacked subtle phrases and nuances. Yet they moved forward when others were physically and mentally exhausted.

Robert E. Lee undertook a job which was too big for one man and for which he was inadequate. But he toiled without complaining, surrendered without equivocating, and died without faltering. He showed that human virtue was equal to, if not superior to, human calamity. His greatest asset was a unique kind of grace. His greatest triumph was the simple splendor of his being.

No phrase-maker like Lincoln, Lee did not leave utterances or messages for school children to memorize and recite. Still, he could be explicit and forceful in word as well as in deed. Consider the words Lee scribbled on a paper which was not discovered until after his death: "The gentleman does not needlessly and unnecessarily remind an offender of a wrong he may have committed against him. He can not only forgive, he can forget. He strives for that nobleness of self and mildness of character which impart sufficient strength to *let the past be but the past.*"

Lee's genius was essentially military; but his greatness was essentially religious. He cannot be understood against a background of politics, philosophy or polemics. All efforts to find Lee's "secret" have failed because they have followed the wrong leads.

Unfortunately, there was no mechanism in nineteenth century Protestant America for handling a saint. The separation of church and state was written into the Federal constitution. The principle had been ingrained in the Virginia conscience by the Jeffersonians. To have used any of the terms of Roman Catholicism would have seemed like a betrayal to the American way of life.

Yet some of Lee's exploits were considered little short of "miraculous." If he did not make the lame walk, he definitely made them fight—and in a land of insurgent nationalism, this counted for more. His sword and his marvelously attractive face would have done well in church iconography or cathedral carvings. He was the southern Saint George slaying Yankee dragons. If one checks the steps of canonization, he will find that Lee has moved far along the road to ultimate acceptance.

The idea would have appalled him. He was, so far as I can discover, truly a humble man. There is about him a soft, winsome quality—not unlike that of Saint Francis. The extraordinary attraction which both of these men exerted over animals is only one of their points of comparison. They had an attraction to, and an attractiveness for, all living things. Literally everything and everybody loved them.

Forget the Lee of battle, and see the old man moving

among Lexington's children. Forget the general in gray, and see the old fellow in the black suit, moving back and forth between his home and his chapel. Focus sharply on this man. For *this* is Robert E. Lee.

BIBLIOGRAPHICAL NOTE

The already massive bibliography of material on Lee and the Civil War has increased so rapidly during the Civil War Centennial that keeping up with it is a full time job. Still, nothing has come out on Lee which matches in quality or detail Douglas Southall Freeman's four-volume *R. E. Lee* (1935-1936). Freeman's "Select Critical Bibliography," IV, 543-569, is indispensable and need not be duplicated here. In 1951, the Bibliographical Society of the University of Virginia published a *Preliminary Checklist of Writings about R. E. Lee* (Library of Congress Card A 52-5027), prepared by William M. Hollis and me. This volume will meet the needs of readers who want to know more of the South's greatest figure.

For official material on the Federal level, one should consult the *Congressional Globe*, which, after 1873, became known as the *Congressional Record*. Here may be found the day-to-day transactions of Congress. The papers of Lincoln, Johnson and Grant are available in James D. Richardson's *Compilation of the Messages and Papers of the Presidents, 1789-1897* (1907). Of special interest during the period covered by this book is the 1866 *Report of the Joint Committee on Reconstruction*. My chapter on "The Hearing" is based on this report.

Over ninety per cent of all extant military papers of Robert

E. Lee are held by the U. S. Adjutant General's Department and the Engineer Department of the War Department in Washington. The Library of Congress has many of his private papers, and the Lee Archives at Washington and Lee University contain a mass of material on the Lexington years.

Lee biographies have been appearing steadily ever since the Civil War. James McCabe's, the earliest extensive one, was called *Life and Campaigns of Robert E. Lee* (1866) and was followed by the works of William P. Snow and E. A. Pollard. The three nineteenth century writers who dealt most effectively with the Southern hero were Talbott Sweeney, John Esten Cooke and Thomas Nelson Page. I have tried to appraise their work in my study of *Virginians on Olympus* (1951).

A seldom explored source of information on Lee's reputation is the group of books by Europeans who were attracted to him. These include Von Achten der Letzte, Justus Scheibert, and Heros von Börcke in Germany; and Viscount G. J. Wolseley, C. C. Chesney, and R. W. Murray in England.

No single study is as winning, however, as Robert E. Lee, Jr.'s *Recollections and Letters of General Robert E. Lee* (1905). This is the one volume I would recommend for the general reader as a beginning point. For those whose taste runs to pictorial material, Roy Meredith's *The Face of Robert E. Lee in Life and Legend* (1947) is a good introduction.

Though covering earlier years than those featured in this book, the recent compilation by Clifford Dowdy and Louis Manarin of *The Wartime Papers of R. E. Lee* (Boston, 1961) opens up new vistas of understanding. Edmund Wilson's *Patriotic Gore: Studies in the Literature of the American Civil War* (1962) replaces all earlier efforts as the standard study of the literary scene.

For a broad panoramic view of Reconstruction, these six books are recommended: Allan Nevins, *The Emergence of Modern America* (1927); Claude Bowers, *The Tragic Era: The Revolution after Lincoln* (1929); J. G. Randall, *Civil War and Reconstruction* (1937); Paul H. Buck, *Road to Reunion, 1865-1870* (1937); E. Merton Coulter, *The South During Recon-*

struction (1947); and Holding Carter, *The Angry Scar: The Story of Reconstruction* (1959). The best short summary in the last few years is John Hope Franklin's *Reconstruction after the Civil War* (1961). The "suggested readings" at the end of the book are helpful and will bring the reader up to the 1960's. The text itself is highly opinionated.

A period so controversial as Reconstruction is subject to constant contention and revisions. Anyone interested in this subject should consult these three basic articles: Francis B. Simkins, "New Viewpoints of Southern Reconstruction," *Journal of Southern History*, VI, February, 1939; Howard K. Beale, "On Rewriting Reconstruction History," *American Historical Review*, LV, July, 1940; and Bernard Weisberger, "The Dark and Bloody Ground of Reconstruction Historiography," *Journal of Southern History*, XXV, November, 1959.

Since so much of the controversy of the 1860's was on the state level, the minutes of the state legislatures, the constitutional conventions, and the reports of occupying officers are critical. On the constitutional issue, see Francis N. Thorpe, *Federal and State Constitutions* (1909). Material available on the former Confederate States is uneven and sometimes hard to come by. Perhaps the best single study is Francis Simkins' and Robert H. Woody's, *South Carolina during Reconstruction* (1932). The more recent study by Hugh T. Lefler and Albert Newsome on *North Carolina* (Chapel Hill, 1954) is notable. Two standard volumes on the Old Dominion are Hamilton J. Eckenrode's *The Political History of Virginia during Reconstruction* (1904), and A. A. Taylor's *The Negro in the Reconstruction of Virginia* (1926).

Most of the Southern states have arranged special reading lists, exhibits, and tours in connection with the Civil War Centennial. Information on these may be obtained by writing the Historical Commission at the appropriate state capital. That problems (especially racial) raised in the 1860's are with us still can be demonstrated by reading the morning newspaper. Now it is the World South, not merely the American South, which is being revolutionized and reconstructed.

INDEX

Adams, Charles Francis, 224
Adams, Henry, 227
Afton Mountain, 62, 66
Aikman, Duncan, 182
Alabama, 169
Alabama, University of, 85
Alabama Association of Base Ball Players, 175
Alexander, Archibald, 77
Alexander, E. P., 211
Alexander, Porter, 192
Alexander, Robert, 76
Amelia Courthouse (Richmond), 12
Anderson, Charles, 91
Andrews, Sidney, 190
Anglican Church, 205, 206, 211-212
Appeal to Arms, The (Hosmer), 182
Appomattox, battle of, 1, 16, 23, 34, 38, 43, 47, 103
Arkansas, 169
Army, Confederate, 5-6, 8-9, 10-12
Augusta Academy, 76

Baker & Lewis, 176
Baldwin, John B., 117
Banks, Nathaniel P., 18

Barnum, P. T., 175
Barton, H. S., 203, 204, 218
Bauregard, P. G. T., 93, 180
Beecher, Henry Ward, 86, 164
Benét, Stephen Vincent, 37, 217
Benjamin, Judah P., 56
Berkeley, William, 150, 152
Blackford, W. W., 17
Blair, Francis Preston, 162
Blow, Henry T., 118-119, 122, 124
Bonaparte, Jerome Napoleon, 94
Bond, Christiana, 171
Bonds, Confederate, 114
Booth, John Wilkes, 42
Borden, Benjamin, 69
Boston *Transcript* (newspaper), 109
Boston *Traveler*, 165
Botts, John Minor, 117, 155
Bradford, Gamaliel, 225
Bradford, William, 225
Brady, Matthew, 36-39, 42, 46, 51, 161
Breckenridge, John C., 71, 196-197
Brockenbrough, Francis, 165-166
Brockenbrough, Jude, 49, 56, 80, 85, 165
Brooks, Noah, 25, 30

[235]

INDEX

Broun, Thomas L., 100
Brown, Orland, 117
Buckingham Courthouse (Virginia), 19
Burnside, Ambrose, 207
Butler, Benjamin F., 4, 157, 191
Button, General, 13
Byrd, William, 150

Caesar (Negro), 166
Calvin, John, 65
Calvinists, 70
Cameron, Simon, 162
Campbell, Isaac, 76
Campbell, Thomas, 1
Cape Fear Academy, 199
Carpet-baggers, 163
Carter, Robert, 205
Carter, Thomas, 52, 101
Caskie, Norvell, 103
Catawba Indians, 64
Catumseh, Chief, 91
Central Pacific Railroad, 175
Chambrun, Marquis de, 21
Chapman, Thomas, 108
Charles II, King of England, 226
Charleston, South Carolina, 5, 197-199
Charleston *Courier*, 198
Charlotte, Columbia, and Augusta Railroad, 190
Chase, Salmon P., 8, 31
Cherokee Indians, 64
Chestnut, Mrs. Mary, 93
Chilton, R. S., 83
Chittum, Charles, 220
Christ Church (Alexandria), 205
City Hall (Richmond), 11
City Point, Virginia, 20
Civil Rights Bill, 125
Civil War, The (Street), 223
Cole, Reverend Mr., 211
Cole, Robert G., 197
Collyar, John B., 168
Columbia, South Carolina, 191-192
Columbine (ship), 196
Compton, James, 176
Confederate Veteran (periodical), 168

Congress, Confederate, 5, 7-8
Congress, United States, 109, 111, 157, 158
Congressional Reconstruction Committee, 110-111, 119, 125
Conkling, Roscoe, 118, 122
Constitution, U.S., 158
Constitutional Union Party, 71
Constitutional View of the Late War between the States (Stephens), 169
Cooper, Peter, 164
Corse, George, 13, 46
Crozet, Claude, 78
Cumberland Courthouse (Virginia), 19
Cunningham, Dr., 186
Currency, Confederate, 3
Custer, George A., 43
Custis, George Washington Parke, 154
Custis, Mary Anne Randolph *see* Lee, Mary (Mrs. Robert E.)

Dana, Charles B., 206
Davidson, Albert, 41
Davidson, Donald, quoted, 17, 48, 62, 74
Davidson, Percy, 203
Davis, Jefferson, 3, 4, 6, 9, 22, 32, 42, 51, 97, 98, 120-121, 180, 207
 capture of, 52
Debt, Confederate, 113-114
Democrats, 188
Derwent (Plantation), 63-64
Dews, William J., 117
Dickinson, J. J., 196
Dixie, 5, 21, 23, 85, 125, 191, 223
"Dixie" (song), 21, 27
Douglas, Robert M., 181
Douglas, Stephen A., 71

Early, Jubal, 56, 92, 180
Ewell, Richard S., 13

Fenton, Reuben E., 164
Fitzhugh, George, 169
Flanagan's Mill (Virginia), 19
Florida, 169, 196-197

INDEX [237]

Ford's Theater (Washington, D.C.), 19, 34-35
Fort Donelson, battle of, 8
Fort Hamilton (New York), 206
Fort Henry (Virginia), 150
Fort Sumter (South Carolina), 5
Fortress Monroe (Virginia), 7
Four Years with General Lee (Taylor), 208
Fourteenth Amendment, 158
Franklin Society, 135
Frazer, Douglas, 163
Fredricksburg, battle of, 47
Freeman, Douglas Southall, 225
Fuller, John W., 79

Gardner, Alexander, 33
Garrison, William Lloyd, 50
Gary, General, 10
Georgia, 4, 169, 193-194
Gettysburg, battle of, 3, 97, 209
Godkin, Edwin L., 25
Golden Horseshoe, Knights of the, 65
Gooch, William, 65
Gordon, E. C., 135
Grace Episcopal Church (Lexington), 57, 70, 142, 178, 203-204, 212-213
Grady, Henry, 224-225
Graham, William, 57, 76
Graham Literary Society, 140
Graham Philanthropic Society, 145
Grant, Ulysses S., 4, 6, 7, 8, 12, 13, 15-16, 24, 25, 34, 168, 171-172, 181
  comments on Robert E. Lee, 91
  pays tribute to Lee, 16
Graves, C. A., 132
"Greatest Show on Earth, The," 175
Greeley, Horace, 164
Guild, Dr., 103
Guild, Mrs., 104

Hampton, Wade, 168-169
Hancock, Winfield S., 41
Harper's Monthly (magazine), 28
Harper's Weekly, 164

Harris, Professor, 144
Harrison, Belle, 82, 103
Haskell, Alexander, 192
Hatcher, William, 2
Hayne, Paul Hamilton, quoted, 36
Hedger, C. W., 140
Helper, H. R., 189
Hill, A. P., 15
Hitchcock, Roswell, 164
Holden, William, 187-188
Homestead Act, 23
Hood, John B., 5
Hosmer, J. K., 182
Hot Springs, 170
Humphreys, Professor, 143
Houston, Sam, 72
Howard, Jacob M., 111-124
Hunter, David, 75-76, 132, 179
Huston, Dr., 186

Illinois *State Journal* (newspaper), 7
Indian uprisings (1865), 43

Jackson, Andrew (Stonewall), 69, 71, 93, 126, 181, 207, 209
James, Army of the, 4
James River, 1, 21, 69, 160
Jefferson, Thomas, 16, 66
Jeffersonian Party, 71
Jeffersonians, 228
John, Saint, quoted, 173
Johnson, Andrew, 8, 41, 42, 52, 58, 109, 112, 117, 119, 126, 156-157, 172, 187
Johnson, Reverdy, 162
Johnston, Joseph, 9, 12, 41, 51, 93, 96, 195
Johnston, William P., 143
"Johnston affair," 162-165
Joint Committee on Reconstruction, 109
Joint Report (bulletin), 124
Jones, J. William, 213, 220
Jordan, John, Jr., 170
Joynes, Edward S., 143
Julian, George W., 50
Junkin, George, 71-72

INDEX

Keith, Ruel, 205
Kennon, Britannia (Brit), 103
Kershaw, General, 13
Kirk, George, 188
Kirkpatrick, Dr., 144
Knights of the White Camelia, 56
Koones, C. M., 219
Ku Klux Klan, 56, 188

Lacy, B. T., 209
Lady of the Lake (Scott), 45
Lafayette Square, Washington, D.C., 26
Land Grant College Act, 23
Land We Love, The (magazine), 126
Lawton, General, 194
Lea, Reyner de, 152
Lederer, John, 64
Lee, Agnes (daughter), 156, 185, 189-190, 192, 195
Lee, Ann (daughter), 93, 156, 184-185, 208-209
Lee, Ann Hill Carter (mother), 152-153
Lee, Carter (brother), 19, 33
Lee, Charlotte Wickham (daughter-in-law), 147
Lee, Custis (son), 3, 13, 131, 160, 218
Lee, Fitzhugh (son), 36, 146-148, 158, 185, 200, 224, 227
Lee, Harold (uncle), 152
Lee, Harry (father), 57, 131, 185, 195
Lee, Henry (brother), 57
Lee, Lionel (ancestor), 204
Lee, Mary (daughter), 48, 49, 208
Lee, Mary (Mrs. Robert E.), 3, 39, 44, 50, 84, 87, 91, 131, 153-155, 156, 168, 174, 200, 203, 205, 206, 217
Lee, Mary Tabb Bolling (daughter-in-law), 146
Lee, Mildred (daughter), 94, 134, 156, 185, 215
Lee, Richard (grandfather), 152, 205

Lee, Robert E.
  accepts field command (1862), 96
  accepts Presidency of Washington College, 58-59
  accused of deserting Army, 162
  appointed Commander in Chief of the Armies of the Confederate States, 6
  arrives in Lexington, Virginia, 74
  attends wedding of son Fitzhugh, 146
  attitudes on college discipline, 141
  attitudes on future of South, 58-59
  attitudes on restoration of South, 136
  attitudes on Virginia, 53-54
  begins restoration of Washington College, 78, 80
  birthplace of, 57
  characteristics of, 37-38, 88-106, 131-134, 165, 176-178, 204, 227-229
  compared with a Cavalier, 105, 167
  death of, 216-221
  declining health of, 161
  family background of, 151-160, 204-205
  fastidiousness of, 131
  growth of legend of, 222-227
  instigates building of chapel at Washington College, 129
  military ability of, 98-100
  moves family to Lexington, Virginia, 87
  offered Presidency of Washington College, 50
  promotes railroad, 182-183
  quoted, 146
  recalls sieges witnessed in Civil War, 149-150
  receives news of daughter Annie's death, 208
  receives unfavorable publicity in the North, 164-165
  religion and, 204-215
  returns to Richmond, 1
  resigns from U.S. Army, 58

INDEX

settles on Franklin Street, 3
summoned before Congressional Reconstruction Committee, 110-127
surrenders to Ulysses S. Grant, 15-16, 25
travels through South, 184-190, 192-201
visits daughter Annie's grave, 189
visits father's grave, 195
visits Grant, 181-182
visits spas with wife, 170-171
writes to President Johnson, 53
Lee, Robert E., Jr., 33, 43, 45, 102, 133, 144, 154, 174, 200
quoted, 88
Lee, the American (Bradford), 225
Lee Chapel Museum, 226
"Lee Kneeling at the Grave of Jackson" (Völck), 181
Lee's Lieutenants (Freeman), 225
Leigh, Mrs. Chapman, 82, 103
Letcher, John, 71, 72, 212
Lexington, Virginia, 68, 70, 74, 75-87, 175-176, 202
Lexington *Gazette*, (newspaper), 79, 84, 108, 109, 110, 125, 157, 175
Libby Prison (Richmond), 2, 11
Liberty Hall, 76-77
Liberty Hall Academy, 77
Lincoln, Abraham, 4, 6-7, 8-9, 13-14, 20-35, 207
assassination of, 19, 35
elected to second Presidential term, 7
signs proclamation closing Southern ports, 29
visits Richmond, 11-12
visits Virginia, 8
Lincoln, Mary Todd (Mrs. Abraham), 22, 24-25, 31-33
Littlefield, Milton, 188
Long, General, 50
Longstreet, James, 96
Louisiana, 169
Lowe, Andrew, 194, 195
Lowell, James Russell, 25
Lynchburg, Virginia, 9, 68

Macbeth (Shakespeare), 21-22
Macrae, David, 134
Madison, R. L., 218
Mardi Gras, 175
Mahone, William, 150
Malvern, S.S. (Union raider), 11
"Marching through Georgia" (song), 190
Marlowe, Christopher, quoted, 128
"Marseillaise" (song), 150
Marshall, Anne Lee, 57
Marshall, George, 93
Marshall, William, 57
Massachusetts Cavalry, Fourth, 11
Maury, Dabney, 158
Maury, Matthew Fontaine, 56

McCaw, Dr., 186
McClain, S. P., 176
McCleary, Harvey, 140
McClellan, George B., 96
McCormick, Cyrus, 69, 109
McDonald, Mrs., 218
McDowell, Irvin, 97
McLean, Wilmer, 16
Meade, George G., 17, 210
Meade, William, 203, 205
Memminger, C. G., 198
Miley, Michael, 180
Milton, John, 196
Minnegerode, Reverend, 9
Minor, Jimmie, 63
Morrison, Dr. Samuel Brown, 170
Mosby, John S., 41, 46, 186
Motley, John L., 181
Mount Vernon, New York, 22

Natchez (boat), 175
Natchez *Democrat* (newspaper), 126
Natural Bridge (Rockbridge), 183
Negroes, 24, 82, 110, 115, 119, 124, 126, 159
suffrage, 169
Newcomb, Warren, 133
New York *Daily News* (newspaper), 109
New York *Herald* (newspaper), 95, 139, 190, 199

INDEX

New York *Independent* (newspaper), 164-165
New York *Times* (newspaper), 134, 164
New York *Tribune* (newspaper), 30, 126, 164
New York *World* (newspaper), 30
Nick King (steamer), 195, 197
Nightingale, William, 195
North, 13, 23-24, 40, 42, 165, 223, 224
  attitudes of the, 123
  war profits in the, 168
North Carolina, 6, 169, 187-188
North Carolina, University of, 85
North River, 69
Northern Virginia, Army of, 3, 13, 38, 73, 99

Ord, General, 4
Order of the White Rose, 56
Ould, Robert, 39, 149
Our American Cousin (play), 33

Parker, John F., 35
Parsons, Governor, 126
Pender, Dorsey, 92
Pendleton, W. N., 57, 70, 81, 82, 142, 178-179, 220, 221
Pepys, Samuel, quoted, 75
Petersburg, battle of, 8, 38
Petersburg, Virginia, 150
Petersburg *Daily Express* (newspaper), 7
Phillips, Wendell, 109
Pickett, George, 186
Pineton, Charles, 21
Poe, Edgar Allan, 150
Politicians, Union, 117
Poor whites, 166
Porter, David D., 11
Potter, Horatio, 179
Powell, J. W., 175
Powers, Stephen, 198
Presbyterians, 65, 70, 78
Preston, Margaret J., 176-177
Protestant Episcopal Church, 212
Pryor, Mrs. Roger A., 103

R. E. Lee (Freeman), 225
Racist groups (1865), 56
Radical Republicans, 154, 188
Radicals, 191
Raleigh *Sentinel*, 188
Randolph, Inness, quoted, 55-56
Randolph, John, 53
Rebels, 5, 24, 124
Reconstruction, 179, 206, 224
Reid, Colonel, 78
Republican Party, 6, 118
Republicans, 109, 188
Rhett, Robert Barnwell, 37
Rhett, Robert Goodwyn, 192
Rhodes, J. P., 176
Rhodes, William A., 80
Richmond, Virginia, 1-3, 5, 6, 52
  desperation and famine in, 10-12
  fall of, 9-14
  surrender of, 11
Richmond *Inquirer*, 199
River Queen (Union steamer), 20, 22, 24
Robert E. Lee (steamboat), 175
Robinson, Graham, 141
Rockbridge Alum Springs, 170
Rockbridge Bible Society, 214
Rockbridge County, Virginia, 69
Rockfish Gap, Virginia, 62, 64
Ruff, J. M., 163
Ruffin, Edmund, 56

Saint George's Chapel (Windsor), 204
St. Michael's Church (Charleston), 198
Saint Paul's Church (Richmond), 9
St. Philip's Church (Charleston), 198
Sandburg, Carl, quoted, 19
Sanderson, Colonel, 197
Savannah, Georgia, 6
Savannah *Republican*, 194
Schoffner Act, 188
Scots, 65
Scott, R. K., 192
Scott, Walter, 45
Secessionists, 116

INDEX [241]

Seward, William, 7, 25-26
Seymour, Horatio, 118
Shakespeare, William, 21-22, 184, 222
Shelby, Joseph, 52
Shenandoah, C.S.S. (Confederate raider), 52
Shenandoah Valley, 62-74
　battle of, 4
　early settlers in the, 64-66, 69-70
　famous sons of the, 72
　folklore in the, 73
　politicians in the, 71
　religion in the, 65, 70
Sheridan, Phillip H., 4, 8, 14, 67
Sherman, William T., 4, 6, 24, 41, 190
　marches on Georgia, 4
Simms, William Gilmore, 191
Smith, Channing, 46
Smith, Francis H., 78, 179
Smith, Kirby, 52
Smith, Lee, 93
Smith, William (Extra Billy), 81, 82
South, 13, 23-24, 40, 50, 58, 109-111, 119, 157, 175, 187
　collapse of the, 6, 42
　post-war brutality in, 157
　post-war despair in, 169
　race relationships in the, 115
　race riots in the, 126
South Carolina, 169, 190-192, 197-199
South Carolina Society Hall (Charleston), 198
Southern Collegian (college bulletin), 138-139
Spanish-American War, 224
Speed, Joshua, 29
Spotswood, Alexander, 65
Stanford, Leland, 175
Stanton, Edwin M., 25
Senate, U.S., debates Lee's resignation from Army, 162
Stephens, Alexander, 169
Stevens, Thaddeus, 51, 108, 109, 111, 118, 156
Stewart, John, 3, 185

Stowe, Harriet Beecher, 86
Street, James, 223
Stuart, Carolina, 103
Stuart, Margaret, 103
Sulivane, Clement, 10, 11
Sumner, Charles, 30-31, 51
Susquehannock Indians, 64
Swepson, George, 188
Syrus, Pubilius, quoted, 108

Tagart, Samuel, 181, 203
Tagart, Mrs. Samuel, 181
Tate, Allen, 14
Taylor, Walter, 36, 53, 92, 93, 208
Thirteenth Amendment, 6
Thomas, Philip F., 162
Tidewater, Virginia, 49, 50, 60, 63
Timrod, Henry, quoted, 169-170
Tinker, Charles, 29
Tractarian Movement, 206
Traveller (Horse), 1, 13, 18, 19, 57, 61, 62, 63, 73, 82, 84, 87, 100-102, 104, 180, 220, 223
Trowbridge, J. T., 193
Tucker, Beverley, quoted, 68
Turner, Josiah, Jr., 188
Turning Stream, The (Aikman), 182

Underwood, John, 155
Union Pacific Railroad, 175
Union Theological Seminary, 164
University of the South (Tennessee), 56, 85
Universities, Southern, post-war problems of, 85

Valentine, E. V., 201
Varner, Andrew, 87
Venable, Charles, 14, 19, 92
Vicksburg, battle of, 8
Virginia, 53-54, 187
　patriots of, 76
Virginia, University of, 56
Virginia Military Institute (V.M.I.), 67, 75-76, 78, 179
Virginian, The (Wister), 43
Völck, A. J., 181

Wagner, Jacob, 166
Wallace, Harry, 220
Warm Springs, 170
Washington, D.C., 8, 20, 24, 110
Washington, George, 9, 22, 65, 77, 93, 205
Washington College, 64, 71, 76, 77-81, 83, 85-87, 88-89, 106, 109, 131, 135-138, 139, 142, 164-165, 167, 173
   curriculum of, 135
   description of Lee's office at, 128-130
   loses financial aid from North, 165
   rebuilding of, 80
Washington Literary Society, 145
Washington *Star* (newspaper), 134
Watchman (newspaper), 134
Weitzel, Godfrey, 11, 24, 31
Western North Carolina Railroad, 188
Whig Party, 70, 118

White, James J., 78, 180-181
White, W. S., 83, 220
White House, Washington, D.C., 26-29, 32, 34
White League, 56
White Sulphur Springs, 170-171
Whitman, Walt, 52, 161
Wickham, Henry T., 226
Willcock, O.B., 163-164
Williams, Martha Custis (Markie), 103
Wilmer, Joseph B. P., 57, 64
Wilmington, battle of, 5
Wilmington, North Carolina, 98
Wilson, Rathmell, 133
Wilson, Woodrow, 193
Wise, John S., 55, 99
Woodruff, Josephus, 192
Woodward, Thomas, 198
Worth, Jonathan, 187

"*Yankee Doodle*" (song), 27
Yankees, 10-11, 24, 53, 81, 82, 99